From the Publishers of Guitar Player, Keyboard, and Bass Player Magazines

THE Musician's HOME RECORDING HANDBOOK

Practical Techniques for Recording Great Music at Home

By Ted Greenwald

GPI Books
MILLER FREEMAN INC., SAN FRANCISCO

GPI Books

Miller Freeman Inc., 600 Harrison Street, San Francisco, CA 94107

Publishers of *Guitar Player, Keyboard,* and *Bass Player* Magazines

ISBN 0-87930-237-2

Library of Congress Catalog Card Number: 92-71022

Copyeditor: Tom Mulhern

Technical artist: Rick Eberly

Designer: Saroyan Humphrey

Cover photograph ©1992 Harold H. Williams

Plug photos courtesy of Mike Harvey, California Switch & Signal, Inc., Gardena, CA

Printed in the United States of America

94 95 96   5 4 3

Contents

3 The Recording Engineer's Palette: Equipment and Techniques

Contents

4 Refining Your Sound: Advanced Techniques

Introduction

➤ When you have a private studio in your living room, basement, garage, bedroom, or closet, you possess what even the wealthiest, most successful recording artists often lack: a music production facility in which you have total creative control. You've selected the equipment. You know how it's laid out and how to operate it. You're not beholden to anyone else's schedule, budget, or taste. The music that comes out is purely your own. In the best case, your home studio reflects your own musical aspirations more directly than any other recording studio possibly could.

This book is designed to help you make that ideal a reality.

The *Musician's Home Recording Handbook* emphasizes concepts that are applicable to any recording situation, from amateur to professional, from humble to grandiose—distinctions that, as the technology develops, become less relevant with each passing year. Comprising columns published in *Guitar Player* between late 1987 and early 1992, it includes large doses of basic information, as well as step-by-step descriptions of advanced techniques. The original articles have been organized, updated, and expanded to cover just about every area of music production, as it is currently practiced. I hope that it will

prove useful to those just getting started in home recording, to those trying to fill in the gaping holes left by even the best background in studio techniques (generally trial-by-fire in a pro studio), and even to musicians who have no intention of recording at home, but would like to understand more clearly what goes on in the studio. Because the book originated with my *Guitar Player* columns, it includes some specific details of special interest to guitarists. However, the principles and techniques are applicable to all musicians who want to make high-quality recordings at home.

Making music is the ultimate goal of recording. Thus, this is a book for musicians, and it assumes a relatively high degree of musical understanding and ability—factors that can be seen as having far more to do with making an effective recording than equipment or technical know-how. If you feel you need to know more about music, you'll find it helpful to give some attention to any of the countless books available covering crucial topics such as theory, harmony, and composition; arrangement and orchestration; instrumental technique and performance; and music history and appreciation. Listening is equally helpful. Although they're less well defined than in music, recording practices and values coalesce into a variety of styles. Simply paying close attention to what's happening on your turntable and radio can be very informative and inspiring.

On the other hand, you don't need to know what you don't need to know. The technical information presented here is basic and to the point wherever possible. Given that the subject matter is, by nature, technology-intensive, a complete presentation could involve large chunks of physics, electronics, and computer programming. I'm not familiar enough with any of those subjects to write about them authoritatively. But take my word for it: They're really not necessary for making great recordings at home.

I've approached writing about home recording with a number of other assumptions that might be helpful to mention. First, I assume that you don't have unlimited financial resources; that you want to save money, or at least to spend it carefully and wisely. However, I rarely mention—and never recommend—specific pieces of equipment. Most of what's available these days is adequate or even perfect for a given set of circumstances; there's no way I can know the particulars of yours. The number of variables, both within a specific piece of equipment and in the context of your needs, is so over-

whelming that a lengthy period of ownership is often the only sure way to tell the diamonds from the turkeys.

Shop carefully and make yourself as fully informed as possible. Buy one piece of equipment at a time, and explore it fully before you buy the next. In time you'll have a dynamite studio. It's inevitable that you'll go wrong once in a while—certainly I still do—but that's part of the learning experience.

As for your time, I assume that you'd rather spend it making music than scratching your head over technical details. I assume, or rather hope, that you're more interested in learning and gaining experience than in recording a hit album on your first try. (If that's what you want to do, hire a "name" producer and let him handle the rest.) I believe that the best way to explain anything is to start on a basic, simple level and work your way up, and that the best way to learn anything is to dive in head-first.

Finally, I assume that your musical vision is valid. If you put your energy into expressing it with sincerity and tenacity, you'll come out with recordings that you can be proud of, regardless of the equipment you use. I ask that you make the same assumption. Best of luck with your recordings.

—Ted Greenwald

Welcome Home: An Introduction to the Home Recording Studio

Philosophy of the Home Recording Studio

➤ It's tempting to believe that you can't make satisfying, CD-worthy recordings at home, especially when you look at the kinds of gear available in pro studios. Sure, a Tascam Portastudio is great for a four-part sketch, but what about all the other tracks you want to lay down? What about great-sounding studio monitors? What about an automated mixing board? What about multiple echo chambers, delay lines, flangers, harmonizers, and gates? And what about all the background noise you have to deal with at home?

All legitimate questions. There's one answer to all of them: Make the most of what you have. That's what any good musician does, and it's what the best professional recording engineers and producers do, as well.

Some compromise between lofty artistic goals and cold, hard reality is part and parcel of the creative process. But keep in mind that what you're compromising is the technology, not the music. There's a saying heard in recording studios across the globe: "The Beatles recorded *Sgt. Pepper's Lonely Hearts Club Band* on a 4-track." They really did—no fooling. Dust off the record (or better yet, the CD—your finished masters are more comparable to it), give it a spin, and try to imagine how they did it. Even 25 years later, it sounds golden.

Of course, that's not quite the whole story. Truth is, the Beatles had access to the best technical minds in the record business at the time, the best arrangers, the best songwriters, and the best players. Okay, so I left out the fact that they had a budget that would have made even the Stones blush—the point is that it wasn't the technology that made the difference. It was a combination of expertise and musicianship.

The question isn't how much gear you have in your living room. The question is, do you want to use the tools at hand to make the best music you can? If you've read this far, the answer is probably yes. That's the thought underlying every chapter of this book, whether it's stated explicitly or not. Don't worry about what you don't have. Learn all you can about recording techniques and technology. Use what you already have to the best advantage and to the furthest capability it offers. And be a good musician. You'll make great tapes, guaranteed.

Today's inexpensive recording equipment is capable of far better performance than most people get out of it, simply because they believe it can't do any better, and because they lack the experience of trying.

Even a couple of portable cassette machines and a cheesy stereo receiver with a collapse-to-mono switch can be used as a multi-track recording system (see Fig. 1-1).

Fig. 1-1. The make-do approach to multi-tracking, using two cheap cassette machines and a stereo receiver with a mono switch: (1) Record track 1 onto cassette machine 1. (2) Route output from cassette 1 to one side of the receiver's auxiliary input. Route sound source to the other side. Make sure mono switch is activated, and connect one side of the receiver's tape output to cassette machine 2's input. Record track 2 to cassette 2 while playing back cassette 1. (3) Switch cassettes and record track 3 onto cassette 1 while playing back cassette 2. Repeat (2) and (3) as necessary.

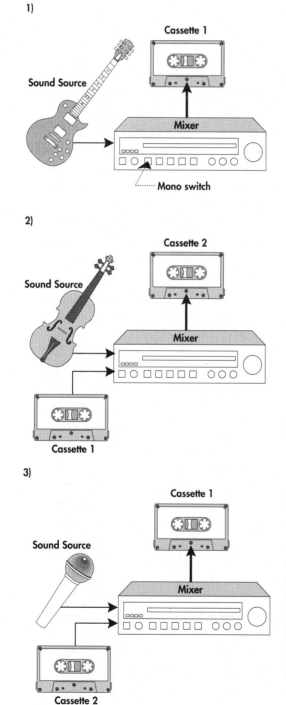

I recommend approaching home recording with a make-do attitude. Of course there are disadvantages to making do—mixes with rough edges, noisy recordings, mistakes necessarily left in—but the make-do attitude has several undeniable benefits. For one thing, you make music, rather than twiddle your thumbs. If you make do with what you already have, you won't go broke as quickly as you would if you were to buy all the gadgetry you think you need—and if you don't have any money in the first place, you'll be letting yourself out of a lot of needless frustration.

But more important, making do tends to focus your attention on coming up with creative solutions to technical and musical problems. You create at a higher artistic level because your attention is focused on the act of creation, rather than on making up reasons why you can't do what you want to do. (If you find this difficult to accept, compare, say, some classic R&B or jazz sides—recorded in one take because there was no other option—and a modern pop production recorded in several studios over the course of a few months. In many cases, the difference in spontaneous energy and artistic focus is distinctly audible.)

Moreover, by making do, you will establish a more personal, individual style, rather than doing things the same ways as everybody else. Ironically, restricting yourself to the materials at hand can free you to have a more individual impact on your productions. At best, this makes for better music; at worst, it makes for better learning. Not a bad deal, either way.

How much or how little you can manage to make do with, of course, depends to some extent on your musical style. Some folks will be after serious demos of their rock and roll bands. Generally, this is going to take more gear than recording a solo acoustic performance for your friends to listen to, no matter how dedicated you are to the make-do ethic. Those who just want an environment in which they can experiment by themselves will have the easiest time making do. So the first thing to do is take stock of your goals.

After you have a relatively clear idea of the extent of your productions and what standard of technical quality you're after—be ambitious here—the next step is to take an inventory of the musical and recording equipment you have. Make a list of everything from the most exquisite guitar in your collection to the wah-wah pedal you stashed away in the closet years ago. If you're working with limited resources and you're at all musically adventurous, everything—*everything*—will come in handy sooner or later.

Think of the equipment in your list as the beginnings of a system. A recording studio is made up of components that play particular roles, like a stereo system that has a separate turntable or CD player, amplifier, and speakers. The components depend on each other to function; to some extent, no one part is useful without the others. Some crucial roles may be unfilled in your current setup, but don't worry about that until you're actually up and running and making music. In many cases, you can do without even the most basic components, or make do with a cheap, simple solution until you're ready to take more drastic action.

In the next few pages, we'll go over the components that may or may not already be in your system. Any that aren't, you'll want to consider doing without, getting, or upgrading as time goes on. Until then—make do. And make great music.

Designing Your System: A Survey of Basic Components

➤ Any recording studio is a system made up of components. What goes into the system depends on a number of factors. First, what components do you already have? You may be able to get right to the music immediately. If not, there may be inexpensive ways to get up and running quickly and easily.

The next most important consideration is how much you're willing to spend. Are you thinking in terms of hundreds, thousands, or tens of thousands of dollars? There's virtually no end to the amount of money you can pour into a home studio, so give yourself a rough budget. You can cut down on expenses somewhat by purchasing used equipment, which is plentiful in these days of six-month product-line lifespans. Buy new if the device in question relies on moving parts, such as tape decks and microphones. Used synthesizers, digital effect boxes, and other all-electronic pieces are a safe bet.

It's also sensible to consider your present level of expertise. The learning curve can be pretty steep, especially if you acquire a lot of sophisticated equipment at once. Regardless of how much you eventually intend to spend, you may find it easiest to start with a small, simple system and add components as your understanding and abilities grow.

What kind of music do you want to make? Recording a string quartet is a different matter from recording a rock and roll band, which is a different matter still from recording a simple guitar/vocal solo or duo. Will you use a drum machine, or are you going to record live drums? Rock recordings may require different equipment than jazz recordings, and one-man synthesizer-only productions have their own technical requirements. Moving in one direction doesn't cut you off from others, so it's helpful to focus your interests as tightly as you can.

What style of working do you want your studio to support? Do you need to provide a room for recording acoustic instruments? A listening environment for clients? Does the studio have to accommodate anyone besides you? More than one person at a time, or more than a few? Will projects be completed in a single intensive session, in which case you can put the studio together one day and take it apart the next? Or will you work on a number of projects in the course of a day, in which case you have to document, catalog, and store various tapes and setups?

Finally, what standard of technical quality are you after? Will your recordings be pressed onto CDs? Broadcast over radio? Heard by record-company A&R people? Distributed as Christmas presents? Played only for close friends? Or are they simply for your own satisfaction?

Basic Components

Having considered these questions, let's take a look at everything your system might include. Along the way, we'll try to point out the potential costs, and the circumstances in which you might want, need, or do without them. Keep in mind that you don't need anything more than the simplest tape machine to make recordings. How many of these components you use depends entirely on your tastes, finances, experience, and ambitions.

Basic Deck. This is the workhorse, used for recording individual parts, or tracks. If you're not going to do any overdubbing—that is, if you will be recording everything live, all at once—this deck should fit the description of the mixdown deck below. Otherwise, this is where the initial recording takes place. (The final mixdown is recorded by a separate mixdown deck.)

For most people, the basic deck is a multi-track recorder of some sort, most likely a four- or eight-track cassette machine. Other options include four- or eight-track reel-to-reel decks in 1/4" or 1/2" formats (the measurements refer to tape width), Akai-style 12-track cartridge machines, and for those who like to live on the techno-

logical and financial edge, a multi-track direct-to-hard-disk digital recording system built around a personal computer. The cost of a basic machine is likely to be between $500 and several thousand clams.

(If you're already starting to have doubts, don't be shy about trying the make-do method outlined in Fig. 1-1. If you're careful, you can make very satisfying recordings that way.)

Mixdown Deck. Your final product, or master tape, will be recorded on this deck. The finished recording will be either a direct-to-stereo (or direct-to-mono) live performance, or a mixture of tracks recorded on the basic multi-track deck. (If you want to go multi-track, the only way to get around having two decks is to do a new mix every time somebody wants to hear your music.)

You can skimp in a big way, if you must, on the mixdown deck. A crummy cassette recorder is adequate if you aren't too choosy about the final sound quality, so dig out that old blaster. The other end of the spectrum is a personal computer-based digital recording system such as Digidesign's SoundTools system or Passport's AudioTrax. The DAT (digital audio tape) format is a truly wonderful development for home recordists. Also in this category are DAT's precursors, digital encoders designed to work with a video recorder (such as the Sony F1), and video machines with digital audio. In between are any number of reel-to-reel decks (preferably in stereo half-track format). A mixdown deck will run you between $25 and a few thousand.

Engineer's Monitor. This lets you hear what's on tape. Preferably, your monitoring system should be isolated from, or at least louder than, the sound you intend to record. Otherwise, you won't be able to tell what's going onto tape until after it's there. (Of course, if it's necessary to get on with making music, the make-do recording engineer can stand not to hear the results until after the take is completed, but it isn't ideal.)

In many cases, a home stereo amplifier and speakers will do the trick. Just be careful not to pump live playing at high volume into a relatively cheap speaker; the transients—sharp, loud attacks—may blow it up. If in doubt, use a compressor, or simply keep the volume low. A single speaker is okay if you're going to be mixing to mono in the end. Failing that, use a pair of headphones, which are useful in any case for gaining a detailed, close-up perspective on a mix. Expect to spend between $10 and several hundred bucks for monitors.

Player's Monitor. The preferred technology for allowing the instrumentalist to hear what's going on is a pair of headphones. If the player and the engineer are the same person, you can dispense with the distinction between recordist's and player's monitors.

If you're recording actual sounds in the air—as opposed to recording "direct" through a cable—headphones are a necessity. If you're going direct, speakers are a much more comfortable option. Headphones run between $20 and $200.

Sound Sources. Here's where you can go totally wild. Anything that makes noise is a sound source. This includes musical instruments (yes, the guitar is a musical instrument), amplifiers, your voice, spare tape players, record players, radios, televisions, delay units set to runaway feedback, telephone answering machines, and for you avant-gardists, coffee grinders and non-stick kitchen utensils.

The percussion pattern in the background of the Four Tops' "Reach Out" [*Reach Out*, Motown 5149] was played on a telephone book and then processed with tape delay. The Eurhythmics beat on a Coke bottle during "Sweet Dreams" [*Sweet Dreams*, RCA, AFL1-4681]. You get the picture. Cost: from absolutely free to the entire contents of your bank account.

Microphones. A decent mike is more or less a must. Get two, if you want to record in stereo. Microphones are the most common way of getting guitars, both electric and acoustic, on tape. You won't need a mike if you record everything direct (which means no vocals either), but keep in mind that in a pinch you can use one of those cheap mikes that come with cheap cassette recorders. They only cost a few bucks (but generally you get what you pay for). The cost of a reasonable microphone is between $30 and several hundred smacks.

Signal Processors. Now we're talking about reverbs, delays, compressors, gates, noise-reduction systems, flangers, choruses, harmonizers, phasers, distortion boxes, wahwahs, envelope followers, ring modu-

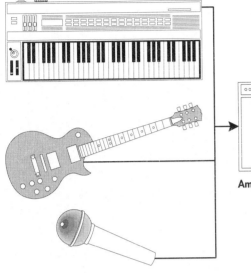

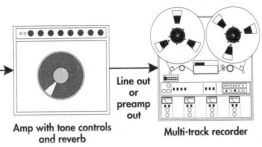

Sound sources

Amp with tone controls
and reverb

Line out
or
preamp
out

Multi-track recorder

Fig. 1-2. Make-do signal processing: You may find it possible to do without reverb units and equalizers. When multi-tracking, route sound sources through a guitar amp with tone controls and reverb. Send the amp's line output (or preamp output) directly to the tape deck. If you're careful with your reverb and tone settings, you can put reverb and EQ on each individual track, rather than adding it during the mix.

lators, and all of that fun stuff. Many home-recording buffs see signal processing as a luxury, but you would do well to consider it essential—particularly reverb.

Fortunately, reasonably good reverbs are pretty inexpensive these days. (A number of companies, such as Alesis and ART, specialize in micro-sized, line-level digital gizmos for home-studio use. Roland, Yamaha, and others make similar multi-effect boxes designed specifically for guitarists). If you don't want to spring for a stand-alone unit, consider recording everything through your trusty Fender Twin Reverb guitar amp or P.A. head, which gives you equalization (tone controls), as well as moderately effective reverb (see Fig. 1-2).

Don't forget that in most circumstances you can use your old stomp boxes for recording—and not just for guitars, but for drums, vocals, weird effects, the works. Cost: $50 to a few thousand.

Mixer. Thanks to the current boom in music-production technology—particularly the proliferation of MIDI synthesizers and samplers—mixing boards that are compact, well-designed for home use, and reasonably inexpensive are easy to find.

A mixer usually serves two functions: getting your instrument signals to the multi-track tape deck, and mixing the recorded tracks into stereo. The more input channels a mixer has, the more instruments you can record at one time, and the more tracks (plus effects such as reverb and delay) you can mix. To maximize a 4-track setup, a mixer with at least six inputs is more or less essential (that's four for the tape outputs, two for stereo reverb).

For better or worse, many readers are bound to have mixers built into their 4-, 6-, or 8-track cassette machines. If so, keep in mind that an add-on mixing board will give you lots of additional flexibility. It's also

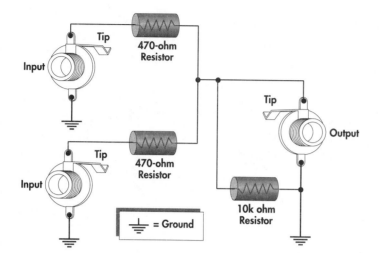

Fig. 1-3. Make-do mixing: This simple home-brew mixer circuit is a superior alternative to mixing through a Y-cable. It can be expanded to accommodate 10 inputs. (Design by Bruce Griffen, Rane Corp. Used by permission.)

likely that you have access to a board used for mixing a band's live performances. This mixer may well be the ticket, so look it over before you buy another.

The absolute low end in this department is a few Y-cables, which cost a few bucks apiece. Owners of 4-track reel-to-reel decks may appreciate knowing that, while mixing via Y-cables isn't exactly sound from an electrical point of view, it isn't illegal, either. In fact, acceptable mixes can be obtained in this way. If you're hard up for finances and not too picky about sound, give it a try. If you're a little more adventurous but just as poor, consider building the make-do mixer shown in Fig. 1-3. A mixer can run anywhere between $200 and hundreds of thousands of dollars.

Cables. Ever notice that cables add hundreds of dollars to your musical expenses? You probably have noticed, and for that reason you're probably forever short on cables. Default on a car payment and forget about the expense: Get millions of cables in all possible combinations of plugs and jacks. Cables fail at the most annoying times, so keep extras on hand. Keep a collection of those little adapters that slip over a plug to change its type—they're a small investment at the local Radio Shack.

It's not necessary to have the highest-quality cables in a home situation, although it's not a bad idea, either. Use good wire, though, wherever cable length exceeds about 10' or so. In general, it's best to keep cable runs as short as possible.

Accessories. This is the catch-all category for all those niggly little things that make life in the studio a little easier. Direct boxes ($40 to $300) convert a high-impedance, high-level signal coming from a guitar, an electronic keyboard, or a drum machine into a low-level, low-impedance microphone signal. If your mixer has channels that offer only mike inputs, these babies can expand the number of useful channels in your mixer, perhaps saving you from having to buy a new board. Microphone transformers ($20 to $60), which do the same thing in the other direction, are worth keeping on hand, too.

Radio Shack sells little amplifier/speakers the size of a transistor radio for about $10. They're great for checking audio signals coming from tape decks, mixer-channel outputs, Walkman cassette players, synthesizers, and so forth. An extra pair of headphones serves the same purpose, and can be helpful from time to time to get a change of perspective while mixing.

You'll need masking tape and felt-tip pens for marking tape reels and boxes, and pads for jotting down ideas and marking tape counter numbers. A Polaroid camera is useful; a snapshot of the mixing board is the poor man's automated setup recall. A stopwatch can be helpful for timing songs and figuring out tempos in beats per minute. Don't forget tape editing blocks, splicing tape, razor blades, and grease pencils (which double for editing tape and marking levels on the mixing board). And the tools and supplies necessary to keep things running smoothly: a spray can of residue-free contact cleaner, a soldering iron and solder, and brass polish for twice-a-year cleaning of all patch cords' ends.

Keep a wish list of things like this, and don't be slack in acquiring them. They can make a big difference when the creativity starts to flow.

Patch Bay. This isn't a necessary item, but it can be extremely useful. Think of it as the Grand Central Station of the studio. In general, all signals, whether they're coming from instruments, effect boxes, or tape machines, should be available at the patch bay to be routed to any input. Signals from tape, for instance, can be routed either directly to the mixer or through a compressor first and then to the mixer.

A well-designed patch bay is the only way to keep control over your system without shutting the door on opportunities to route the signal in unusual ways. It's not recommended for everyone, though. Those who would rather find one way of plugging everything in and never move a thing will be much more comfortable ignoring some of the flexibility that a patch bay provides. There's no shame in that, as long as you're happy with the music that comes out the other end.

Computer and Software. Why a computer? These days, a more likely question is why anyone would want to do without one. The uses multiply every day. A computer can help you keep track of projects, clients, and contacts. It can make tidy forms on which to log such things as multi-track tapes, processor settings, patch configurations, and mixing-board setups.

Computer-based digital recording systems are proliferating, some of them offering four independent tracks, some at a relatively low price. If you're into synthesizers, sequencer software can multiply the number of tracks you're capable of fitting into a mix, and improve the quality of your recordings. There are also hardware/software combinations that let you record and play back fader motions during a mixdown—a high-end application, but perfectly viable for a home setup.

If you're a composer, there are lots of programs to help you out, from notation programs to automated composition utilities to SMPTE time-code event processors. With a modem, you can jack into the world of networks and bulletin boards, bringing you into contact with musicians across the globe to trade information, solve problems, and share sequences and sounds. Admittedly, these sorts of things are still of limited interest among guitarists, but probably not for long. The price of a computer and associated hardware: $600 to $10,000.

Synchronizer. You'll probably need some kind of synchronizer if you intend to link the playback of a tape deck, video deck, drum machine, sequencer, and/or computer. A sync box is a must for composing to video—which a surprising number of musicians are, these days—in order to make particular musical events occur at particular moments in the film. If you're into synthesizers, a tape-sync generator/reader makes it possible to record synthesizer tracks into the sequencer and play them back in sync with guitar, vocal, and other tracks on tape.

Sophisticated tape-sync devices are surprisingly inexpensive these days, starting at around $250. An honest-to-golly SMPTE-to-tape machine synchronizer can cost as much as $4,000, although prices are dropping on these, too.

Workspace. It all fits into this dingy, stuffy little room.

It's important to have enough space, or at least to properly organize what little space you have, so that everything is reachable without too much effort and without too many other things in the way. Make the space as comfortable as possible—the long hours required to make good recordings pass more smoothly this way.

If you plan to record groups of players with full monitoring, or to do extensive overdubbing, you'll need one room for the main studio and another for the control room. (That's the way the pros do it.) A bathroom or living room adjacent to the studio can serve this purpose nicely. In many cases, though, a single room will suffice.

Acoustics are significant, but you can't really expect people to rebuild their houses to accommodate a studio. Clap your hands in various parts of the room and listen for the rebound. If you hear a distinct ping, put down a rug or hang a some curtains. Soundproofing is another matter entirely. It's nearly impossible, and very expensive, to keep loud sounds from getting through the walls of your studio. Obviously, the more soundproof your workspace is, the happier your family and neighbors will be. On the other hand, if they're enjoying the music, you're less likely to run into trouble.

The Production Process, Step by Step

➤ One of the joys of having a studio in your living room is that it frees you from the kinds of discipline that are crucial to making successful recordings in a professional studio. If you feel like putting three weeks' worth of 10-hour days into guitar overdubs, nobody's going to tell you that it's not in the budget. Got a case of the munchies? There's a refrigerator down the hall, and it's stocked with exactly the things you normally eat. When you wake up at 4:00 in the morning with a burning desire to reinterpret "Purple Haze" in Renaissance counterpoint, the studio is ready for business.

In a home situation, the usual production process can be mixed up, recombined, and twisted in all directions to suit your whims. This is proper and good, encouraging an atmosphere of sheer musical adventure that's hard to maintain when dollars are slipping away at a rate of a few hundred an hour. Amid such a ruckus, it's easy to forget that there are logical phases through which a recording generally passes on its way from mental flicker to the top of the charts. If you have a clear sense of how your production is progressing—what stage it's at and what the next step(s) might be—you'll find that the inevitable chaos can be directed toward making the best recordings possible.

So let's run down the process of recorded-music production. Admittedly, dividing things into discrete steps makes for a rather conservative formulation. In recording—in general, and especially at home—the steps are merged, reordered, repeated, and otherwise obscured, but they occur nonetheless, and each offers special musical opportunities. The foundation of this discussion is the idea that recording is an extension of the traditional musical functions of composition, arranging, and performance. It is not a different thing entirely; it is a distinctly *musical* (as opposed to technical) activity, and it has implications for your music as basic as the more traditional aspects of harmony, melody, and rhythm.

Composition. This is the first step, the foundation of the production. You need a song, a riff, a groove, a chord progression, a melody, a texture, an intriguing sonic gesture—an idea that can sustain further development and articulation.

Multi-track tape makes a very convenient and flexible compositional sketch pad. For one thing, it's immediate. Improvisations are captured instantly for further processing, such as transcription or overdubbing. Four tracks can be used to compose separate instrumental parts (drums, bass, chords, melody) or for formal sections (intro, verse, chorus, coda). You can record tracks in rough form, add a few more polished tracks, and replace a rough track with a revised version, *ad infinitum*. If you become adept at tape editing, you can record jammed rehearsals and edit them into structured masterpieces.

Amid all this space-age fun, don't forget pencil and paper. Working out an arrangement on four lines of staff paper can be extremely helpful in forming a clear idea of what it is, precisely, that you hope to create. Once it's all on paper (and in your head), it's a lot easier to get it onto tape.

Rehearsal. For the purposes of recording, rehearsal has become all but obsolete. Multi-tracking makes it possible to record take after take until you get it right—to rehearse as you record, actually, and to convert a rehearsal into a finished take by sheer fiat (and the occasional punch-in). It's also possible to compose and arrange one track at a time, so nobody knows what the notes should be until they're on tape—how can you rehearse parts that haven't yet been composed?

While these methods can yield wonderful results, rehearsing in the traditional manner remains the surest way to make a viable record. Great performances of great material can make up for the most glaring technical deficiencies in a recording. Ideally, your production technique will become fluid enough that you can move effortlessly between a more traditional, big-picture approach and studio-induced spontaneity.

Arrangement and Orchestration. Yet another traditional disci-

pline is supplanted by multi-track tape. With tape, you can hear the arrangement as you create it, evaluating decisions on the basis of how they sound in the air, rather than in your mind's ear. Inevitably, this atrophies the aural imagination, but it makes arrangement and orchestration a far more interactive, real-time process. It's a trade-off that many recording artists make with great success.

Basic Tracks. When you're working with a band, it's standard procedure to begin with "basics," usually a live performance by the rhythm section alone (often with a rough vocal). This forms a skeleton over which overdubs can be laid. If, on the other hand, you operate as a one-man-band, there may be no distinction between basics and overdubs.

In any case, the foundation of the production is usually established during basic tracking. This is a good time to nail, once and for all, the music's style, groove, form, harmonic structure, and overall energy level. If these aspects of the music are utterly clear after the basic tracks are finished, it's much easier to work on fine points of arrangement and orchestration during overdubs.

Overdubs. Any tracks added after the basics are considered overdubs. These usually begin with additional rhythm parts such as strummed guitars and keyboard pads, move on to coloristic features such as percussion, and end with such essential parts as lead vocals and solos. There's no compelling reason to do things in this order, except perhaps that a featured musician is more likely to deliver an inspired performance if the backing tracks are complete. Background vocals often come after the lead, so that they can match the solo vocalist's phrasing.

Even with only four tracks to work with, there's no end to the number of overdubs you can add (when you run out of tracks, you can always bounce). It becomes a point of discipline to avoid going overboard. Critics sometimes refer to this as *overproduction,* but it's more like overarranging. That's one good reason for sticking with a predetermined arrangement. You can always add another few parts if something seems to be lacking.

Mixdown. Some musicians overlook the mix phase because it seems, at that point, like the music has already been made. Actually, the mixdown is like a filter through which the audience hears the performances, and it can have an enormous influence over what they hear and how they hear it.

At the most basic level, the mix puts various musical elements in perspective, so that incidental details aren't distracting and the essential features stay in focus. The mix also serves to integrate the performance, to transform a bunch of tracks into a living, breathing band, and to provide a sense of spatial relationship between instruments.

As Jamaican dubmasters and hip remix producers have demonstrated, the mixing board is a powerful musical instrument and compositional tool in its own right. Wedded with the magic of digital signal processing, it can be used to reshape a piece of music from the ground up. It's become quite common to use the mixdown as the final stage of composition, disassembling the tracks and reconstituting them like Tinker Toys in order to produce a new arrangement and, occasionally, a new piece of music entirely.

Mastering. After you've completed a number of songs, you might want to prepare them for copying to a medium in which they can be distributed to listeners—usually cassettes, but sometimes CDs or vinyl disks. This preparation is known as *mastering.*

The goal of mastering is to create a production master, a final tape from which all subsequent copies will be made. When you're operating out of your living room, it's common to skip this step, making cassettes for friends and family by copying your final mixes one song at a time. After the sixth or seventh copy, however, this can get a little old.

If you mix to an open-reel format, it's a simple matter to compile your masters onto one reel. Use leader or blank tape to edit in a satisfying amount of silence between songs. The proper amount of space to leave between songs varies with the context. Some songs seem to call for a breather when they're over, while others tend to jump right into whatever comes next. In some fields, such as advertising, it's common practice to butt one piece of music up against another, leaving no silence at all. If your final mixes reside on cassettes, you might want to copy each song in the proper order to a production master cassette from which you can run copies.

It's likely that mixes of different songs won't be entirely consistent in their overall tone and volume level. Some are bound to be boomier than others, some brighter, some more hissy. A folk song recorded at 0dB may sound outrageously loud next to a kick-ass boogie that peaks at the same level. This kind of thing can make the difference between a haphazard presentation and a slick package, so consider correcting such disparities during mastering.

You can fiddle with EQ and volume settings as you run each distribution copy, or you can create a trouble-free production master by copying your final mixes one by one, adjusting as you go. After copying each song, roll back and listen to the segue to make sure one flows into the next in a satisfying way. If you only have one mixdown deck, DAT makes a perfect intermediate medium for this kind of work. You can copy to DAT with all of the adjustments you want, and then copy from DAT back to your mixdown deck with minimal degradation of the sound. The DAT copy then serves as a perfect archival

copy that you can duplicate any time you want to put the song on another production master.

Packaging. An optional step, but worth some attention, packaging inevitably influences the attitude with which a listener will approach your music. If you hand-write your labels, the implication is that you're presenting an informal copy. A slick, three-color display makes you look like some kind of a professional. If you adorn the box with a picture of a guy with a nose ring, people will express surprise upon discovering that you're a new ager. It's only natural.

Distribution. Although it can exist in a perceptual vacuum, music doesn't really come to life until people hear it. It's a pain in the neck to bring one's productions to the ears of an attentive audience, but the rewards are invaluable. These include an education in the psychology of listening (that is, the relationship between what you hear and what others hear), loads of useful information about how others make their music, invaluable practice in accepting criticism gracefully, and—it goes without saying—the joy of touching someone with your music. That's something no musician can afford to do without.

Your Studio's Two Greatest Assets

➤ As technomania continues to sweep the musical community like wildfire, the price of staying in the game—or at least maintaining a decently up-to-date home studio—creeps relentlessly skyward. So it's curious that the most crucial two pieces of equipment in your studio are also the least expensive.

Your music is only as good as these little items, and yet every musician is issued a pair of them, free of charge, upon entry into this here paradise. Yes, it's your ears that will ultimately make or break your home productions. Keep them in tune, treat them with respect, and be sure you know what to do with them when the record button is lit.

Speaker Placement. In order to get your ears to do their job right, you have to make sure they're getting accurate information. That is, make sure your monitor speakers are positioned in such a way that you can really hear what's going on. This may sound obvious, but I've worked at well-equipped studios in which the speakers were too close, too far away, too high, angled in the wrong directions, or simply placed at different distances on the right and left.

The optimal position for monitors is at the two points of an equilateral triangle formed by the speakers and your head. They should be at ear height and angled inward just a bit

so that they're pointed directly at your head. You want to hear as much sound directly from the speaker, and as little sound reflected from walls and ceilings, as possible.

Listening. All right, so you've got the speakers properly positioned and you're listening intently. Now—what are you listening *to?* Well, to different things at different phases of the production process.

When you're getting basic sounds to record to multi-track, you should be listening for definition, fullness, consistency of volume, and of course performance quality. Any frequency ranges that seem to be jumping out should be brought under control using equalization or microphone placement, and any gross unevenness in volume level should be either compressed or remedied by the performer.

When you're preparing a mix, listen for balance, both of the levels of various instruments (adjusted at their faders) and of the various timbral colors (adjusted using EQ). You should also be attentive to the placement of the instruments, both back-to-front (determined by a combination of reverb amounts and fader levels) and left-to-right (controlled by the pan pots).

During mixdown, you should be listening for basic problems such as distortion, and for such mistakes as forgetting to turn up the guitar solo. You may want to listen once through for each instrument, and then a few more times for the ways in which various instruments interrelate.

Once the mix is finished, it's time to turn off your analytic mind and listen simply for sheer musical impact. Using your ears in this way involves listening to several aspects of the music simultaneously and judging them as you listen. If you find that it's hard to focus your ears on a number of things at once, make a checklist and listen several times through, once for each thing you want to attend to.

If you're working alone, make sure you give yourself an opportunity to listen—without doing anything else!—at each step in the production process. Roll the tape while you're getting your basic lead sound and listen to it before you record the first take. While you're overdubbing, record a scratch mix after each good take (keep your cassette machine at the ready for this at all times) and listen to it without playing the next part. Give your ears a chance to do their job.

Care and Feeding. As with any aspect of music, practice makes perfect. Training yourself to listen is an important part of being a musician and, like playing and composing well, making good recordings requires its own special listening skills. Fortunately, getting your ears in shape for the studio is as simple and enjoyable as listening to music.

A good place to start is snare drums. Whenever you hear a pop tune, pay attention to the level, attack, fatness, and heaviness of the snare, and make mental notes so that you can compare various sounds from memory. In your own productions, try to emulate the snare sounds you like best. (Sorry to say, if you're recording a real drummer rather than a drum machine, you've got your work cut out for you.) Try the same exercise on other generic instrument sounds: acoustic guitar, bass, various electric guitar types (clean, sustained, fuzzed-out, etc.), kick drum, lead vocal, background vocal(s), and so forth.

If that's too easy, listen for ambience—the stuff going on in the background that contributes to the sound, but isn't played by anyone. For the most part, this will be reverb, delays, and gating effects. Most modern pop productions employ several ambient fields simultaneously; there might be one kind of reverb on the vocal, another on the rhythm guitar, a gated chamber on the snare drum, a long delay trailing behind the vocal or the lead guitar, and so on. (It may help to visualize the sounds as taking place in a surreal space, much like a Dali painting in which common objects, their textures altered in strange ways, are strewn across a vast expanse.)

Ambiences of this kind may be mixed so subtly that you're unlikely to hear them unless you really know what you're listening for. The more familiar you are with this sound-behind-the-sound, the more creative you'll be with effects in general, and the more complete your mixes will sound.

Finally, listen to records for their overall sound—their depth, density, variety (or lack thereof), hue, dynamics, energy, and other abstract qualities. Such things tend to result not from one specific production or instrumental technique, but from the totality of the studio's resources. These qualities will settle into the back of your mind and become an integral part of your musical signature in much the same way that the various styles of playing you learn become assimilated into your personal instrumental voice.

Ear Fatigue. With all of this focused listening, you'll do well to get into the habit of giving your ears a rest from time to time as you work. Ear fatigue is well-known, and well-feared, among recording professionals. They guard against it in two ways: by listening to the music through different sets of monitor speakers (not often practical in a home studio, but worth considering) and by listening over a range of levels.

If you like to blast the rhythm track while you're overdubbing, take it easy every hour or so and go for a few takes with the volume down. Changing the monitor levels frequently is particularly important during the mixdown phase, when it not only reduces ear fatigue, but helps you get the overall sound into perspective.

The Fletcher-Munson Curve. While we're on the subject of monitor levels, there's an interesting fact about volume levels and human anatomy called the Fletcher-Munson Curve. The Curve shows that we hear low frequencies accurately at high listening levels, but less well at quiet levels. In fact, the loudness switch built into many stereo amplifiers and receivers is designed to compensate for just this effect; when you're listening at a soft level, you turn on the loudness, which boosts the lows by approximately the amount that your ear is missing them.

So if you tend to listen at low volumes while you work, you may be overdoing the bottom end. Likewise, if you tend to monitor at apocalyptic levels, your mixes may sound wimpy to someone who prefers to listen more quietly. When you're mixing, keep old Fletcher-Munson in mind and find a good compromise for your bass level and low-end EQ. Or, remember to turn on the loudness switch whenever you turn down the volume. (Incidentally, in my studio, the analog mixdown deck distorts a bit, emphasizing the lows—a common problem. I've found that monitoring with my amp's loudness button on encourages me to go a little easy on the bass. The mixdown deck adds it back, so the low end comes out about right in the end.)

Trust. One of the most critical aspects of using your ears is psychological. Like a psychiatric patient learning to feel comfortable with a new shrink, you must learn to trust your ears. This may sound easy, but when the VU meters are pinned in the red, it's hard not to dump what your ears say in favor of what your eyes are telling you.

But if it sounds good, who cares what the meters look like? And if it sounds *great,* it's foolish to risk screwing it up by adjusting things until they look right. The same goes for fader positions, EQ settings, delay times, and so on, ad infinitum. If it sounds good, do it.

The job of the eyes, basically, is to guide the ears and double-check them. Of course, there are times when it's best to let your eyes take over altogether—though always under the benevolent supervision of the ears. One is when you're recording individual tracks to multi-track, without any premixing or effects. In this case, you want a clean, noise-free signal on tape so that you have maximum flexibility later. So watch those meters!

Another time to heed what your eyes are telling you is during the final stages of a mixdown. You've marked all of the fader levels and effect-send amounts—for which there might be any number of changes, or "moves," as the song plays—and you're trying to push the faders up and down without making a mistake. At that point, your ears should already have done their job, and you should feel free to concentrate on executing the moves accurately and with conviction. You can always listen after you've gotten through a good take.

As you work with your ears, it's helpful to keep in mind that there's a huge subjective component to listening. Four months from now, you can be sure that the mix you did today will sound very different, and yet your favorite records sound the same every time you hear them. The point is that making music and enjoying music involve different kinds of ear-work. You have a different psychological relationship with your own music than you have with that of Jimi Hendrix—you accept his, but you're more likely to question your own. Likewise, those who listen to your music will accept it if it conveys your confidence in your artistic vision.

That's when all the listening pays off.

What's A Producer?

➤ In any recording session, there are at least three sets of shoes to be filled: those of the musician, the engineer, and the producer. In most home studios, the musician, the engineer, and the producer are the same person, so it helps to have a working knowledge of all three roles. Knowing when it's appropriate to step into which shoes, and what to do while you're wearing them, can make your recording sessions more productive.

This book assumes that you stand in the musician's shoes quite often, and is mostly oriented toward telling you how to put on those of the engineer. But the producer's role is something of a mystery. What, exactly, does a producer do? The general outlines are fairly clear, but even among music-industry insiders, there's no single idea regarding what, specifically, the producer's job is. Before we get caught up in the complexities of engineering, let's take look at how a producer can contribute to the success of a recording project.

The Big Picture. The producer's most basic function is to keep an eye, and an ear, on "the big picture"—a concept of what the recording should, ideally, sound like. Most of what goes on during a recording session requires great attention to detail, but while a session is in progress, the producer deliberately steers clear of most of it. While the players are concentrating on the notes and the engineer is capturing the sounds, the producer stands back and makes sure that each detail is contributing to the whole.

Organizing Sessions. A productive recording session often requires planning. Based on his big-picture conception, the producer has a clear idea of the technical parameters of the project—from tape formats to the number of cassette copies to be run off at the end of the day—as well as the creative parameters, including style, instrumentation, and the degree of professionalism to be achieved. Thus, he's in the best position to organize the sessions.

The choice of studio is an important one. In a home-studio situation, this might translate as the choice of equipment—is the usual complement of gear sufficient for the job, or do you need to buy, rent, or borrow more? Ditto for the musicians involved: Does the band need to hire a percussionist or bring in a vocalist? If so, who's the right person for the job? Is the band even ready to record? Sometimes a few leisurely hours spent rehearsing, composing, or writing out parts can save a lot of session time.

Taking these factors into account,

he books sessions accordingly. It's his responsibility to make sure everyone knows what will be expected of them, and then to see that everyone delivers.

Budgeting Money and Time. The finances available for a given project must be divvied up among various necessities: hired musical talent, blank tape, rented gear, transportation, perhaps even meals and phone calls. Then, the budget has to be met—or more money acquired.

Time and money are virtually identical in a professional studio; even though time is "free" at home, it's still often in limited supply. The producer allocates time among various tasks (basic tracks, overdubs, mixdown, and tape copies) so that they can be completed by the time the session is over. He also has a hand in keeping things moving along steadily, so that time-consuming trivialities—say, trying out a new gadget—don't obscure more important issues, such as getting a great guitar solo.

Getting Good Performances. Although the players are responsible for the nuts and bolts of performing the music, it's the producer's responsibility to see that their talents are used effectively.

One very important thing he can do is to make sure that their needs, both personal and technical, are met, so that they can work without distraction. The producer can also play an inspirational role, psyching up the players and keeping their energy levels high, focusing their attention on the essential aspects of the music as

they perfect their takes. He can also help by fostering an atmosphere of cooperation between musicians, engineers, record-company people, and other interested parties—good studio etiquette in any case.

Most important, it's his job to recognize a great take when it comes along. He should be familiar enough with the musicians' capabilities not to let them get away with a lackadaisical performance (within the constraints of the time allotted, of course). On the other hand, many a musician has been run into the ground by a producer who kept pushing for another take long after the best one had been played.

Musical Focus. This is the part of the producer's role most familiar to the public at large. Producers are often associated with a "sound," or with an approach to the recording process that lends their recordings an identifiable style. Some take the attitude that their job is to bring out the best and most personal in a performer. Others assume that their role is to make a hit record, regardless of the performer's ideas or abilities.

Regardless of such points of personal style and philosophy, the producer can perform a very valuable service by mediating among competing interests, such as the drummer who thinks his snare drum needs to dominate the mix, the keyboard player who thinks his pad should be front and center, and the record-company executive who only wants to hear a retread of this week's Top 10.

The producer's musical contribution may be large or small, depending on the requirements of the project. It may involve something as subtle as making sure the sound of the recording is stylistically consistent with the music. On the other hand, it may be as drastic as rearranging a song, changing its tempo, manipulating its form, and rewriting the chorus. (Many producers, having discharged their organizational responsibilities, are content simply to read the newspaper.)

Entrepreneurship. It's often up to the producer to steer a project from the studio toward its intended audience. The stylistically astute producer knows the market well enough to get the recording into the hands of people who can make it a commercial success.

If the recording is a demo, the audience is a club's management or a record company's A&R department. In this case, the producer may play a large role in the packaging and presentation of the tape. If a record company is already involved, he often acts as a liaison between the executives and the artists. Once the recording is slated for release, he oversees the mastering session and approves the master from which records, cassettes, and CDs will be manufactured.

Can your recordings do without a producer? Probably. But if you make music for any purpose besides your own pleasure, or if you are on a limited budget of time or money, you might find it worthwhile to begin every project by lacing up the producer's shoes and taking a good, long look at your goals and resources. Scribble a few notes on the producer's pad, make a few phone calls, and gather the necessary supplies. You just might find that you're more productive when you finally strap on your guitar, slide into the musician's slippers, and start making music.

How Recording Works: Basic Concepts

How Sound Works

➤ Regardless of what equipment you use and what style of music you make, the basic stuff of your recordings is sound. The evanescent substance of sound has wonderfully mysterious qualities. A sound that lasts only an instant can have profound emotional effects. Though immaterial, it can appear to be infinitely nuanced. It's awesome to contemplate that the entire daunting and delightful edifice of music, in all its glory and variety throughout all ages, is built of sound and very little else. Yet most musicians know little about it.

If you intend to capture sound on tape, you can't ignore its structure and properties. Tape machines, signal processors, speakers, amplifiers, and the other tools of the studio are designed to act in a friendly manner toward sound, but they do a better job if you're good with the introductions. And in order to do that, you have to know sound pretty well yourself.

At first glance, the following discussion may seem overly technical, but it all boils down to a few essential concepts that aren't too difficult to grasp. Consider it an initiation into the arcana of musical knowledge.

Good Vibrations. Sound is nothing more than vibrations in the air, fluctuations in air pressure. Whenever the air molecules in the vicinity of your ears compress and decompress (or *rarefy*) very quickly, your eardrums vibrate in sympathy, and a sound appears.

Based on the way air moves, all sounds have three basic aspects: *loudness,* conventionally called volume (or *amplitude*), *pitch* (or *fundamental frequency*), and *timbre* (pronounced "tam-ber," and equivalent to *harmonic frequency content* or *overtone structure*). Loudness, pitch, and timbre refer to human perception, which is to say, to qualities relating to music. The alternate names (amplitude, fundamental frequency, and harmonic frequency content) refer to the same phenomena in the language of physics. As a science, physics describes sound as a pattern of energy, or *waveform,* rather than in terms of human perception.

Loudness. A sound's loudness, or amplitude, corresponds to the force of vibrations in the air—the more energetically the air moves, the louder the sound. Loudness has a secondary aspect that's particularly important in music, *duration.* That is, all sounds rise out of silence and fall back to silence, lasting a specific amount of time. That amount of time is their duration.

Fig. 2-1. The basic back-and-forth vibration of a guitar string creates the fundamental frequency. At the same time, similar back-and-forth vibrations occur along the various divisions, or harmonic nodes, of the string. These create harmonically related overtones that, modified by the instrument's shape and materials, produce the guitar's characteristic timbre. The waveform that represents the guitar's sound is the sum of these vibrational components.

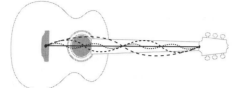

Pitch. Pitch (or lack thereof) is determined by the rate of vibration, the speed of back-and-forth motion as air molecules compress and rarefy, which physicists call frequency. If the compressions and rarefactions happen regularly between 20 and 20,000 times per second, the sound takes on a recognizable musical pitch. Think of the low buzz of a hummingbird's beating wings; to make such a sound, it must flap its wings at least 20 times per second. If the motion of air molecules is irregular, moving back and forth without any discernible pattern, the result is sound without a definite pitch. Generally, unpitched sounds are referred to as noise (although it's not advisable to mention this to your drummer friends).

Frequency is measured in *Hertz* (Hz), or *cycles per second,* with each back-and-forth motion in the air considered a single cycle. Vibrations slower than 20 Hz, and faster than 20,000 Hz (also called 20kHz, or *kilo-Hertz,* meaning thousands of cycles per second), simply don't register with the human ear. Be sure, though, that lower and higher frequencies exist—your dog certainly hears them. The range of all possible frequencies, from infinitely low to infinitely high, is known as the *frequency spectrum.* The part of it that humans can hear, conventionally between 20 Hz and 20kHz, is called the *audio spectrum.*

Timbre. Any single pitched tone can be said to possess a *fundamental frequency.* That's the basic pitch mentioned above, the one you hear when you pick a note on your guitar, based on the length of one cycle of the waveform. Within each cycle, though, there may be subcycles that can be viewed as higher frequencies mixed in with the fundamental. These are called *overtones* or *partials.* Their presence and relative strengths largely determine the character of the sound, its tone color or *timbre*—whether it's bright or dull, shrill or mellow, rough or smooth, or the like.

The overtones in a pitched sound are also known as *harmonics* when they fall into a specific mathematical pattern, called the *harmonic series,* in relation to one another. Consider what happens to a guitar string when you pluck it (see Fig. 2-1). The basic back-and-forth vibration of the entire string creates the fundamental frequency. At the same time, similar back-and-forth vibrations occur along the various divisions, or harmonic nodes, of the string. These create harmonically related overtones. The waveform that represents the guitar's sound is the sum of these vibrational components, modified somewhat by the resonant properties of the instrument's shape and materials.

Unpitched sounds are different only in that there is no recognizable fundamental, and the overtones fall in a random arrangement rather than conforming to the harmonic series.

Generally, a sound's fundamental frequency is a great deal louder than its overtones. If the overtones are very quiet, then the sound is muted and dull. If the highest overtones are loud relative to the others, then the sound is bright. In the natural world, the topmost overtones tend to be the least loud, and they get louder as you move down the frequency spectrum toward the fundamental.

Waveform Graphs.
All of this can become quite apparent when we examine a sound graphically. The most useful ways of doing this are to plot amplitude against time, and to plot amplitude against frequency. Let's start with amplitude against time (see Fig. 2-2).

This kind of plot produces a graphic display of the sound as a waveform. The height of the wave represents the sound's general loudness or volume level, and the number of times it crosses the horizontal axis while maintaining a recognizably repeating shape represents the fundamental frequency. Note that the horizontal axis tells you how much time we're looking at (in this case, a fraction of a second). The wave's overall shape corresponds to its harmonic content, which we hear as timbre. It's nearly impossible to evaluate the precise harmonic content of the wave from this sort of graph, or even the way it

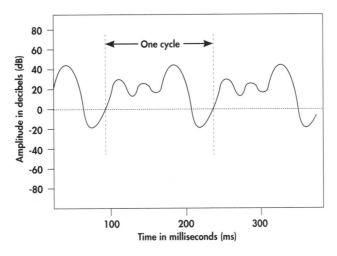

will sound to the ear. The one generalization that seems to hold is that the more jagged the waveform, the stronger the harmonic components.

The other kind of graph, amplitude against frequency, offers a different perspective (see Fig. 2-3). Since time isn't involved in this graph, you might consider it a snapshot representing an instant frozen in time. This representation very clearly illustrates a sound's harmonic contents—the frequency components of which the waveform in Fig. 2-2 is a composite. You can see that the fun-

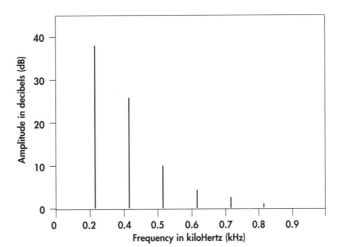

Fig. 2-2. Amplitude plotted against time. The height of the wave represents the sound's general loudness, and the number of times it crosses the horizontal axis represents the fundamental frequency. Note that the horizontal axis tells you how much time is represented. The overall shape of the wave corresponds to its harmonic content, which appears to the ear as timbre.

Fig. 2-3. Amplitude plotted against frequency. This representation illustrates a sound's harmonic contents—the frequency components of which the waveform in Fig. 2-2 is a composite. The fundamental frequency is by far the loudest, and the upper partials taper off into silence.

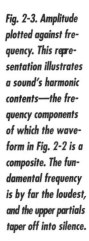

damental frequency is by far the loudest, and that the upper partials taper off into silence.

The Dynamic Nature of Sound. Despite the hard-and-fast look of graphic representations of sound, remember that it's nearly always in motion. Just as the fundamental notes played by a guitarist change over the course of a solo, the associated partials are in motion, as well. A plot of the first few moments after you pluck your guitar will look very different from a plot representing the moments before the sound dies away.

Thus, whenever we speak of a sound's harmonic or frequency content, it is a necessarily general discussion. The most precise we can get is to take the average harmonic content over a period of time. This might be a very short period, such as the time it takes for one cycle of a waveform—which is always changing, of course—with a fundamental frequency of 440 cycles per second. Or, it might be a long period of time, such as a few seconds.

Nonetheless, it helps to get into the habit of visualizing the sounds that come out of your studio in terms of their physical characteristics, and to match these up with musical values that are important to you. Ultimately, your job is to create the waveforms you want to create, and preserve them through the tortuous process of recording. Giving sound this kind of close-up examination is a good first step.

Turning on the Faucet: Signal-Routing Basics

➤ When you crank on the faucet in your kitchen, water starts to flow from the tap. The same thing, more or less, happens when you pick a string on an electric guitar: The vibrating string excites the pickup, and an electrical signal flows from the instrument's output. By connecting a cable to the output, you can route the signal to your mondo Marshall stack.

This simple idea—signal routing—becomes crucial the moment you switch on a tape recorder. In a home studio, where signal-routing resources are likely to be on the paltry side, a solid understanding of signal flow can give you a handle for getting around the limitations of your equipment.

The cable carries the guitar signal to its destination, the amplifier's input, just as the drainpipe below the sink carries the water to some nasty creek on the edge of town. Therein lies the Golden Rule: *Signals flow from outputs to inputs*. Simple, huh? Yes, but it's tempting to try to connect inputs to outputs, and outputs to outputs (a particularly bad idea) when you don't know what you're doing.

When you run into a signal-routing problem, always start by looking for the *source(s)* of the signal, the output(s). Then find the *destination(s)*, or input(s). Finally, find the shortest or most convenient way to connect the two.

A Problem. What kind of problems are we talking about? Try this on for size: You're a member of a band called Cream (and not half-bad with a guitar, to boot). The prehistoric technology you have to work with only allows you to record on four tracks at a time. There are five mikes on Ginger Baker's kit (snare/hi-hat, kick, floor tom, and two overheads for the cymbals and rack toms), a mike on Jack Bruce's bass amp, and a couple on your rig. That's a total of eight sources (outputs from mikes). Since the mixing board has 16 input channels, you're in business.

But how to get the whole thing onto four tracks of tape? If you route the signals from the mixer's direct outputs (the outputs from each channel) to the tape recorder's line inputs, you'll only be able to record four mikes at a time (see Fig. 2-4). We're going to have to mix some of the mike outputs so that we can get them all onto four tracks. Beyond that, we have to do it in such a way that we're left with a reasonable amount of flexibility to

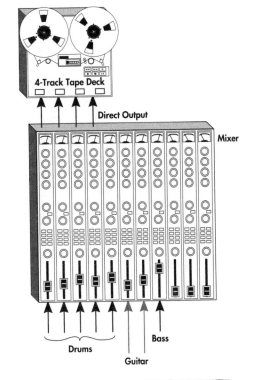

Fig. 2-4. This setup allows only the four mikes to be recorded. The tape deck's inputs are occupied, and the other instruments can't be routed to it from the mixer.

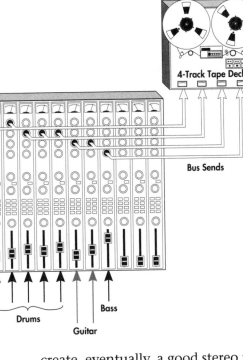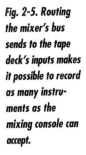

Fig. 2-5. Routing the mixer's bus sends to the tape deck's inputs makes it possible to record as many instruments as the mixing console can accept.

create, eventually, a good stereo mix of the four tracks.

Solutions. To do this, we'll use a nifty feature on the mixing console

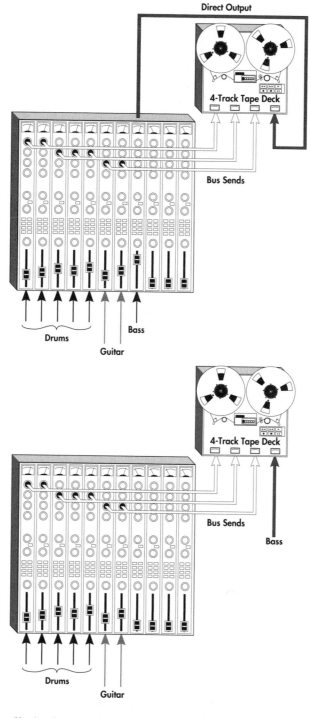

Fig. 2-6. Using a combination of the board's direct outputs and bus sends.

Fig. 2-7. The more direct the connection, the better the sound. This arrangement eliminates the board's electronics in the signal path between the bass and the tape deck.

destination (in this case, the tape deck). If you have four buses, you can use one to mix the kick and snare to one track, the second to send the rest of the drums to another, the third to send the guitar mikes to track three, and the fourth to route the bass to track four (see Fig. 2-5).

On second thought, in this situation we might as well route the bass to the tape deck from its mixer channel's *direct output* (see Fig 2-6). This is more efficient, since the signal doesn't have to travel through a bus to get to its destination. In general, less electronics means less noise and signal degradation, so any time you can avoid routing through a cable, component, signal processor, or whatever, do it.

Looking at the situation once more, it's clear that we might as well bypass the mixer altogether and route the bass mike directly to the tape deck's input—that is, if the deck can accept mike-level signals (look for inputs labelled "microphone"). The routing scheme shown in Fig. 2-7 eliminates everything between source and destination but the cable, so it's guaranteed to give us the cleanest sound possible.

called a *bus send*, also called an *effects send* or an *auxiliary send*. A bus allows you to send signals from any of the mixer's channels (in this case, any combination of mikes) to a single

More Problems and Solutions.

Here's another signal-routing problem. You want to put a slap-back delay on a taped rhythm part, and since the guitar is an old Fender Mustang, it's also going to need a little EQ. (There's no EQ on your board, so you have to use an outboard unit.) One routing scenario goes like this: tape out to delay unit in, delay out to equalizer in, equalizer out to mixer channel in (see Fig. 2-8).

Having listened to the entire mix a couple of times, it becomes clear that the slap should come way down during the verses and up during the choruses. It would be nice to have in-dependent faders for the guitar and the delay. Here's an alternative routing scheme: tape out to mixer channel in; and delay out to equalizer in, equalizer out to another mixer channel in. Now—how to get the guitar signal to the delay? Once again, a trusty bus send comes to the rescue (see Fig. 2-9). Now you can send either the guitar alone, or the guitar and the snare, or any other combination, to the delay. Case closed.

Or, perhaps not. If the delay were noisy and you wanted to use the EQ to get rid of some of the hiss, this would be a great routing arrangement because the EQ is affecting only

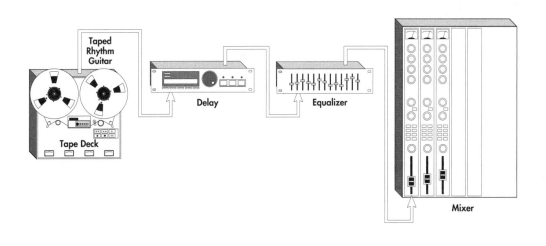

Fig. 2-8. An instrument's signal can be routed through processing devices before being fed into the mixing board. The processors will be exclusive to that particular instrument.

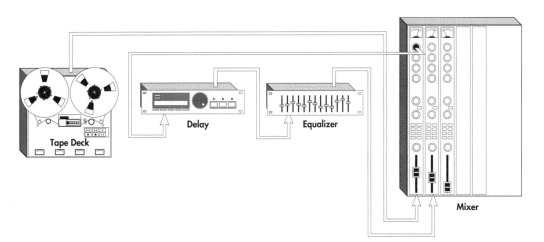

Fig. 2-9. Using a bus send and return (or an input channel) for signal processors provides independent control over the processed signal's volume. It also offers the most flexibility, since any number of instruments can make use of the processors.

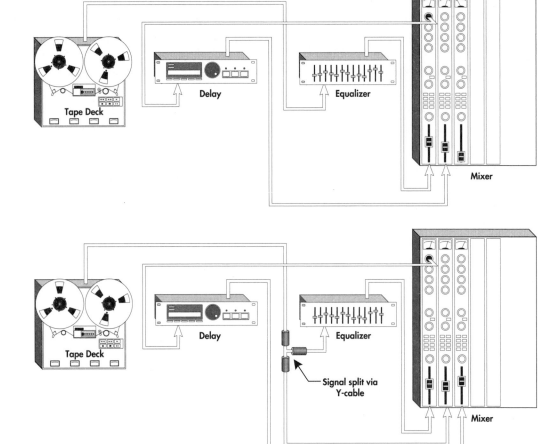

Fig. 2-10. If you want to EQ only the delay's output, use the setup in Fig. 2-9. However, it might be necessary to EQ the instrument before it reaches the delay, in which case this routing scheme is better.

Fig. 2-11. A Y-cable can be used to give you the option of using either processed or unprocessed versions of an instrument's signal.

the delay unit's output. The problem is that, while the guitar's slaps are perfectly EQed, the guitar itself isn't. We've got to process the guitar's output with EQ *before* it gets to the delay; then both the undelayed and the delayed versions of the guitar will have the same EQ. Re-route the signal paths as in Fig. 2-10: taped guitar out to EQ in; EQ out to mixer in; and delay out to another mixer channel in. When you send the signal from the guitar's channel to the delay via the bus send, it will be properly EQed.

One additional complication, if you'll allow. While we were going through all this rigmarole, you decided that maybe—just maybe—you like the sound of the EQed slap with the unEQed guitar. You'd like to give yourself the flexibility to switch between the EQed and unEQed versions of the guitar as you mix, so that you can listen to the two in context and choose the right one. The solution, in this case, is to split the guitar signal. A simple Y-cable will do the job. The routing is the same as before, except that the tape deck's output goes into the single end of the Y-cable. One side of the Y-cable's output goes to a mixer channel, while the other side is treated as the tape out was before (see Fig. 2-11).

Know Your Options. In any situation, there are bound to be a number of signal-routing options, some better than others. Familiarity with the concept and with your system's inputs and outputs will make it easy to find the option that best suits your needs. Having on hand a variety of cable lengths with different combinations of plugs, tons of plug adapters, and a few Y-cables can allow you to maximize your system's potential.

Splitting and Mixing

➤ In the midst of the discussion of signal routing, we brushed up against two crucial concepts: splitting and mixing. When we used a Y-cable to solve our signal routing problems, we were *splitting* a signal into two identical signals, or rather sending the same signal down two separate paths. In studio lingo, the Y-cable was functioning as a *mult,* creating multiple versions of one signal. When we combined signals coming from various microphones onto a single track of tape, we were *mixing* the signals.

Let's take a deeper look into the nature of splitting and mixing, and then cover a few of the factors that can make or break your signal routing schemes.

Splitting. It's the nature of electricity to be splittable. Practically speaking, you can divide an output as many times as you want, sending it to as many destinations as you need to.

A useful item to have in any home studio is a bank of jacks, all of which are connected together. Called a *mult box* (see Fig. 2-12), this is just an overgrown, multiple-output Y-cable. Plug an output into any one jack, and that signal is now available at the other jacks. It doesn't matter what kind of jacks they are—in fact, you can mult together several jacks of different shapes and sizes, and the box will serve as an adapter for various kinds of plugs. (You should be aware, however, that different kinds of plugs are often used for different signal levels, impedances, and so forth, which means that it isn't always useful to route them just anywhere—but we'll get to that later.)

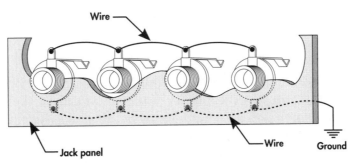

Wire

Jack panel

Wire   Ground

Fig. 2-12. A basic mult panel.

Mixing. You might look at mixing as splitting in reverse. To mix two or more signals together, you ought to be able to plug them into a mult box or Y-cable, and get a composite output from the remaining jack(s), right? Unfortunately, the answer is no.

Electricity, tricky stuff that it is, isn't so kind when you try to merge signals of constantly fluctuating amplitudes, frequencies, and impedances, as signals generated in your studio are likely to be. You will get an output from the remaining jacks, and it will be a composite, but it will be a somewhat distorted composite, a little squirrelly in level and frequency contents. In other words, it will be a low-quality version of the signal you're trying to create. Proper mixing requires the proper circuitry—the kind built into mixing boards.

Rules. All of which leads to two simple rules: (1) You can split a signal by dividing the wire it's travelling down, and (2) you can't mix signals just by running their wires together, at least not without causing distortion.

If a Y-cable or a mult box is the only mixing tool you have at your disposal, then by all means use it—but be aware that it's less than ideal. In fact, if the levels you're dealing with are particularly high, the mult method can fry your gear, so be careful. Line, mike, and instrument levels (which are what guitars, tape decks, preamps, synthesizers, and mixers deal with) should be okay.

Most of what you do in your studio will be various combinations of mixing, splitting, and routing. Your job is to make sure the various signals get to where they're supposed to go, and that they sound good when they get there—that they aren't too distorted, haven't picked up a lot of noise along the way, and generally sound right to your ears.

Signal Levels, Impedances, and Balancing

➤ Recording engineering isn't called engineering for nothing. A lot of technical understanding goes into the design of your equipment, and at least a little should go into operating it. Considering the complexity of the music production process, though, making great recordings on modern gear requires very little specialized background. A few decades ago, it was necessary, literally, to be an engineer in order to avoid all of the pitfalls inherent in capturing sound on magnetic tape.

Today's home recording equipment is designed to be fairly idiot-proof. (That's not meant as any insult to those who are finding it rough going!) Level standards have been developed so that most equipment is intercompatible, as long as you don't push it beyond reasonable limits. Plug formats have evolved to the degree that, to some extent, you have to go out of your way to connect inappropriate sources and destinations. Integration and automatic switching have eliminated many of the old setup hassles. Effects that used to require complex signal-routing schemes and hours of adjustment are now available at the touch of a button. And the audio quality is good enough that you don't have to jump through hoops just to get a decent sound. What a playground!

Nonetheless, a few variables remain that can cause trouble if you're not on the lookout for them. For the most part, they boil down to levels, impedances, and balancing. Keeping levels under control is the trickiest, but that's a big part of the game of recording anyway. The others will usually take care of themselves, but it's worth knowing that they may become an issue from time to time.

Levels. Different kinds of audio equipment are designed to operate within specific ranges of amplitude, or *signal level*. Some operate best in a higher range, some in a lower range. Of course, levels are influenced by the height to which you push up a fader or gain pot, but such effects are secondary to the overall level at which the gear is designed to operate best.

In this context, the term "level" refers to a piece of equipment's standard operating level, the level in *decibels* (dB) at which it can be considered to be putting out 0 VU (volume units). For the moment, consider 0VU to mean "high enough above the noise level of the equipment to sound good, but not so high as to cause distortion." The decibel is a unit for measuring loudness. A Volume Unit is an equivalent measure that serves for representing decibels on a *VU meter*.

The basic standard operating levels are referred to as *line level, microphone level,* and *instrument level*. Their definitions aren't set in stone, having resulted from a combination of physics, engineering, commerce, and habit, all intertwined. For practical purposes, though, they can be summarized as follows:

Line Level. There are really two "line levels," one for professional gear and one for "semi-pro" gear such as home-recording equipment. Most semi-pro gear (4-track tape decks, small mixers, stereo amplifiers, cassette decks, and so forth) is built for a line level of -10dB. That is, -10dB = 0VU. (When a VU meter sees a level of -10dB, it reads 0VU, which is somewhere in the middle of the meter. If the level drops by 1dB, the meter will read -1VU. Likewise, if the level rises, the meter registers an equivalent rise.) Pro gear of the kind you'll find in a recording studio—monster consoles, 24-track tape decks, high-end outboard effects, and the like—put out and accept a line level of +4dB.

If you send a measly little -10dB

signal from your Tascam mixer's effect send to a fancy Lexicon 480XL reverberator that's designed to operate with signals in the +4dB range, the reverb won't have much to work with. It won't be able to work out its mathematical calculations at full resolution, its output will be very weak, and you'll have to crank it up so high that it will probably be too noisy to use.

On the other hand, if you send a +4dB-standard output from a pro tape deck to a channel of your -10dB-standard mixer, you won't have to turn the fader up very high before you pin the VU meter and the mixer starts distorting. Fortunately, many effects units and semi-pro mixers these days are being built with -10/+4dB switches at their inputs and outputs.

Incidentally, it may look like the difference between -10dB and +4dB is a cool 14dB, but that's not the case. The scales in which the two line levels are measured aren't the same. The -10 figure is referenced to volts (dBV), while +4 is referenced to milliwatts and impedance (dBm). Don't sweat the difference, though. The former is still lower, and the latter higher.

Microphone Level. In order to pick up subtle sonic details, the diaphragm of a microphone—its ear drum, if you will—must be sensitive enough to respond to the most minute variations in air pressure. Given the tiny scale of the diaphragm's motion, the levels it generates are very low. Thus, a microphone's standard operating level is around -60dB. That's one of the rea-

sons why you need a transformer to plug a low-impedance mike into a line-level mixer input; the transformer steps up the mike's level. It's also why a mixer's mike inputs usually include a preamp.

Instrument Level. This is what comes out of your guitar, as well as old-fashioned keyboards such as the Fender Rhodes piano and the Hohner Clavinet. (Synthesizers, drum machines, and the like usually put out semi-pro line level.) Instrument level is higher than mike level, but still pretty low, somewhere around -40dB.

Since manufacturers of stomp-box effects expect you to plug your guitar directly into them, they're built to operate in this low range. When you send a signal from your -10dB mixer's effect send to a stomp box—which is a perfectly reasonable thing to do if you want to make the most of your equipment—you should expect to keep the send level way down so that you don't distort the stomp box. Some units are more tolerant than others of this sort of abuse.

Impedances. In a home studio, there's not much reason to be concerned with impedances. Most of the low-impedance equipment you run into in semi-pro studios, usually microphones, uses XLR connectors. It will work beautifully when plugged into virtually any XLR-style input. Mixers and DAT tape recorders that offer the option of using either RCA or XLR connectors operate at line level, but their impedances won't present a problem.

High-impedance equipment

usually sports a 1/4" phone plug that may well be suitable for your mixer's line-level input channels. Plugging a high-impedance mike into a line input may or may not give you enough level to work with, however. If not, a direct box or a preamp is in order.

The only way to route a low-impedance mike into a high-impedance input such as a line input, or an instrument's high-impedance output into a low-impedance XLR-style mike input, is by going through a transformer. Low-to-high-impedance transformers are known as *direct boxes*. Devices that work in the other direction are usually called *impedance-matching transformers*.

If you're ever in doubt about whether you can use a particular mike with a particular input, keep in mind the following handy dandy phrase: "Low into high will fly; high into low won't go." That is, check the impedance specs for the mike output and for the mixer input. If the mike specs out lower than the mixer, you're in luck. Otherwise, look for some other solution.

Balancing. If you rarely stray from home, you don't have to worry about whether a given piece of equipment is electrically *balanced*. Balancing protects the quality of the audio signals running around the studio, and requires a connector with three contact surfaces such as an XLR plug or jack. Home studios are usually 100% unbalanced, give or take a microphone or two. Signals in professional studios, on the other hand, are balanced to the degree that it's possible.

Balancing is a nifty electrical trick that keeps noise out of an audio system. It works like this: The output signal is split into two wires. One wire's signal is reversed in phase. As the two signals travel down their two parallel wires, any muck that manages to get into them—radio signals, AC hum, noise, and the like—is identical. On the receiving end, the phase-reversed signal is corrected (that is, reversed again), putting it back into the proper phase. Any noise picked up along the way is now in phase in one wire, out of phase in the other. When the two signals are mixed back together, the out-of-phase noise cancels out the in-phase noise. *Voila,* a noise-free signal, compliments of the wonders of physics.

In order to plug a balanced output into an unbalanced input (or vice-versa), it's necessary to terminate the phase-reversed wire properly. This requires either a direct box or impedance-matching transformer, or an adapter cable wired to match the phase polarity of your balanced gear. (Consult the manual if you're building such a cable yourself, or your vendor if you're buying one.) As with semi-pro and pro line levels, both unbalanced and balanced connections are found on an increasing number of mixers and amplifiers that straddle the line between professional and hobbyist applications.

Don't Worry, Be Happy. If all of this seems like a lot of technical details to attend to, don't worry. In most cases, you won't hurt anything by mismatching levels, impedances, and so forth. You will, however, encourage the two gremlins of audio production, noise and distortion, to creep into your productions.

Try to keep track of what kinds of audio signals you're dealing with at all times, and try to use them sensibly. This will cut down on the number of audio mysteries you run into in your work, and will certainly improve the quality of the sounds you end up with.

The Technology of Analog Recording

➤ The technical aspects of recording may seem like a lot of needless details, but they're well worth a bit of attention. Knowing how it all works can help you to use your equipment more effectively, keep it in good working order, and figure out what the problem is when you run into trouble.

For instance, when you understand the role played by the magnetic particles that coat one side of a length of audio tape, you're more likely to spend a few extra bucks on high-quality tape that holds a good, strong signal and doesn't shed its oxide. You're liable to keep your deck's heads free of stray oxide particles once you know that electricity must jump across a tiny gap in playback and record heads. Having a grasp of the relationship between tape speed and recorded pitch frees you to create super-fast leads, super-low bass lines, super-heavy snare drum sounds, gong sounds from crash cymbals, and a multitude of other effects.

With that in mind, let's take a look at recording itself: what it is and how it works. But first, a word from our sponsor—the muse of our art form, Calliope.

Is It Live Or Is It...? Recording involves translating sounds into a medium in which they can be stored. Playback simply reverses the process, retrieving the translation and converting it back into something that resembles the original sound. *Fidelity* (meaning faithfulness) is the word we use to describe the precision with which this feat is achieved. *High fidelity* means that the sound has been translated accurately, stored with minimal degradation, and retranslated accurately.

The implication, at least for recording, is that under ideal circumstances the listener shouldn't be able to distinguish between a "real" sound and its recorded counterpart. This is a worthy goal—if realism is what you

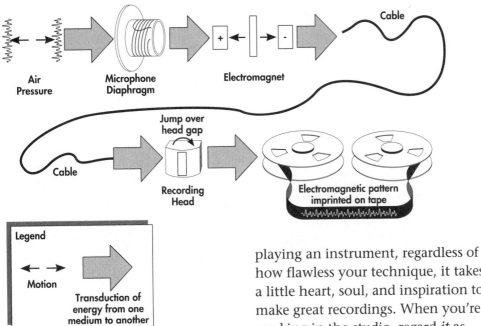

Air Pressure

Microphone Diaphragm

Electromagnet

+ −

Cable

Jump over head gap

Cable

Recording Head

Electromagnetic pattern imprinted on tape

Legend

← →

Motion

Transduction of energy from one medium to another

want to achieve. But if you look at what goes on in a modern recording studio, particularly in popular music, you'll find that in most cases the goal is not to reproduce reality. Rather, it is to produce an illusion. The illusion may be that certain players performed as an ensemble rather than in successive overdubs, that the performance took place in a spacious hall rather than a dank, little room, or that the singer could carry a tune at all. Since the advent of multi-tracking and, recently, digital signal processing, the illusion often takes on a surreal cast. Singers accompany themselves, and various sounds occur in several contrasting spaces simultaneously.

The potential to create something out of nothing makes recording a creative medium somewhat on the order of playing an instrument, rather than simply a technical skill. And, like

playing an instrument, regardless of how flawless your technique, it takes a little heart, soul, and inspiration to make great recordings. When you're working in the studio, regard *it* as your instrument, and play it with the highest level of musical involvement that you can muster.

But enough philosophy—let's move the discussion from the abstract to the concrete.

Storing The Pattern. What we perceive as sound is actually a pattern of fluctuations in air pressure. Thus, in recording, the trick is to find a way to capture and store the pattern so that you can recreate it later. Magnetism turns out to be the ideal medium: A pattern of magnetic fluctuations can be passed over a piece of tape coated with iron oxide particles, and the particles will line up in an analogous pattern and remain that way for years.

The technology that does this is ingenious (see Fig. 2-13): When the air moves in front of a microphone, it pushes and pulls on a very sensitive membrane inside the mike known as the *diaphragm*. The di-

Fig. 2-13. Analog recording: Variations in air pressure, which we hear as sound, push and pull the microphone's diaphragm. The diaphragm, in turn, pushes and pulls a coil of wire between the poles of a magnet, transducing the sound into electromagnetic fluctuations. These are carried through a cable to a tape deck's record head, where the electrical charge is forced to jump over a tiny gap. As tape passes over the head, the magnetic particles that cover its surface are polarized in a pattern analogous to that of the electromagnetic fluctuations. The sound is now recorded on the tape.

aphragm is attached to a magnet that moves, in turn, back and forth between the two poles of an electromagnet, creating a disturbance in the magnetic field.

Thanks to the miracle of electronics, the fluctuations in the magnetic field are carried (via the flow of electrons) through a network of wires to the *record head* of the tape recorder. The head simply passes the electrical current along, but with one wrinkle. Once in the head, the current encounters a tiny gap in its construction called, appropriately, the *head gap*. At this point, the current jumps the gap and continues on its merry way.

When a length of recording tape, which is covered with magnetic particles, passes by the head, the electrical energy that's jumping across the gap realigns the particles according to its strength, which is constantly changing. (Therein lies the importance of keeping your tape deck's heads clean: You wouldn't want all that electricity to trip over an oxide particle, would you?) In this way, the pattern of magnetic fluctuation, which is derived directly from the sound itself, becomes imprinted in the alignment of the oxide particles on the tape.

Applications. The faster the tape moves, the larger the surface available to capture fluctuations in the magnetic field from moment to moment. That is, the faster the tape moves across the record head, the more accurately the magnetic pattern will be imprinted on the tape, and the better your recordings will sound.

You can verify this if your machine gives you two speeds. The faster speed (usually double the slower speed) always sounds better, often so much better that it's worth using up twice as much tape.

The fact that the standard tape speeds are multiples of each other (1-7/8 ips and 3-3/4 ips for cassettes; 7-1/2 ips, 15 ips, and 30 ips for open reels; ips is short for *inches per second*) has a musically useful byproduct. Recorded pitches play back exactly one octave lower at the next-slowest speed to the one at which they're recorded, and one octave higher at the next-fastest speed.

In fact, this is how Alvin and the Chipmunks were able to sing in tune with the backing track. While the track was playing at a slower speed, they simply sang their parts an octave low and half as fast. With the track back at its original speed, the Chipmunk voices were in time, up to pitch, and imbued with that mellifluous rodent-like quality.

If the idea of sounding like Alvin doesn't particularly inspire you, consider creating some impossibly fast lead breaks by recording your backing tracks at your deck's highest speed and the leads at a lower speed. Of course, you'll have to perform them at half tempo and an octave too low, but they'll burn when you crank the tape speed back up. Rolling off some top-end EQ can help take the inevitable "chipmunk effect" out of sped-up tracks.

Alternatively, you might play bass licks on your guitar by recording at the faster speed and playing back at the slower speed. This technique is even more useful for creating unusual textures, such as slowed-down snare drums (bold and trashy) and flutes (which sound like forlorn mutant trombones). Just about anything takes on interesting characteristics when it's played back at a slow speed.

Simple tape-speed manipulation can yield a number of other useful effects, as well. Don't be afraid to experiment: Change speeds while you're recording. Re-record pitch-shifted sounds at still lower (or higher) speeds. Push and pull (gently) on the reels of your reel-to-reel deck, or try to slip into record/play while the machine is in fast-forward. You might come up with something unique.

The Big Playback. Once a sound has been encoded on tape as a pattern of magnetic fluctuations, it's a simple matter to reproduce it. Simply reverse the process.

Pass the tape across a *playback head,* which generates an electrical current analogous to the magnetic pattern on the tape. This current turns on and off an electromagnet, which moves a larger magnet, which is connected to a rather large diaphragm known as a speaker cone. The cone moves back and forth, compressing and rarefying the surrounding air in much the same way as it moved when the original sound occurred. The original waveform (pattern of air compression and rarefaction), which was stored in the form of an analogous electromagnetic flux, is now once again a living, breathing sound.

The Metaphysics of Multi-Tracking

➤ We've seen how sounds are encoded in the alignment of magnetic particles on a length of analog tape, and then decoded for playback through a speaker. If you want to record only one audio channel (mono), it's simple to imagine that you would align the full width of the tape to a single pattern. But what if you want to record a right and a left channel simultaneously (stereo)? In this case, you would divide the width of tape in half—using, in effect, two half-width record heads—and record one pattern on each side.

Extend this idea, and you enter the realm of multi-track recording. If your tape deck records more than one simultaneous track, the record and playback heads must provide a head gap for each track. The tracks run the length of the tape in parallel,

Fig. 2-14. Tape tracks are recorded in parallel. In order to record and play back several tracks, the tape deck's heads must have one gap for each track.

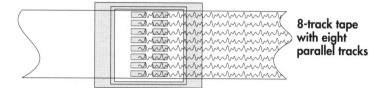

8-track head with eight head-gaps

8-track tape with eight parallel tracks

so the head gaps are stacked one right on top of the other—a column of two for a stereo deck, 16 for a 16-track, and so forth (see Fig. 2-14). The standard for professional analog recording is to encode 24 audio signals side by side on a 2" width of tape.

As long as you want to record them all at the same time, recording several tracks is little different from recording one—several audio signals jump over several head gaps, leaving several parallel magnetic imprints on the tape. The problem crops up if you intend to record on one track while listening to another, a procedure known as *overdubbing*. Some home multi-tracks, particularly the latest generation of cassette decks, use automatic switching to make overdubbing simple and painless. If you use such a machine, you won't have to know what's really going on until you graduate to a higher-end deck. If you use a pro deck or an older semi-pro reel-to-reel, though, you can't avoid the problem inherent in overdubbing. Either way, it's worth knowing how your tape deck works, not to mention what it's doing behind your back.

Three Heads Are Better Than One. So what's the problem? It has to do with the fact that different

heads are involved in recording and playback, and that any given point on a tape can't be in contact with both at the same time.

Heads are arranged across a tape deck's head stack in a strict order, which you can remember as *ERP: erase, record, playback*. The erase head comes first, on the left side, so that previously recorded tape is fully erased before you attempt to record something new. The record head, which turns incoming signals into magnetic flux, is in the middle. The playback (or *repro*) head comes last, on the right. It translates magnetic fluctuations on the tape back into audio signals.

Now, imagine listening to one track while you record another. Since the tape passes over the record head first and then goes on to the playback head, the track(s) you're listening to will always be *late* in relation to the track(s) you're recording (see Fig. 2-15).

I suspect that many readers have accidentally run into this phenomenon already. In fact, if you listen to the track you're recording *as you record it*, you can't help noticing that the sound of your guitar is way behind your fingers. This, too, may be familiar—that feeling that your fingers are getting tangled up because

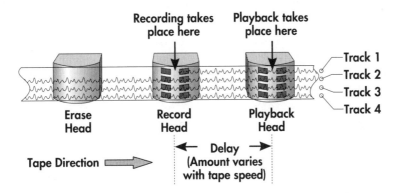

Recording takes place here

Playback takes place here

Track 1
Track 2
Track 3
Track 4

Erase Head

Record Head

Playback Head

Tape Direction ⟹

← Delay →
(Amount varies with tape speed)

Fig. 2-15. Overdub-bing track 1 while monitoring three previously recorded tracks: The playback head reads record-ed material after the record head. Thus, the material being recorded is early in relation to the playback head. This discrepancy is resolved by moni-toring from the record head, rather than the playback head, while over-dubbing.

you're hearing everything you play a fraction of a second late. When the tape moves at 30 ips, as it would in a pro studio, the delay is just slightly noticeable. At 15 ips, it's pretty un-comfortable to play along with. At 7-1/2 ips (not uncommon for home reel-to-reel decks) or slower (in the case of cassette decks), it's unbear-able.

Clearly, monitoring (that is, listen-ing) from the playback head doesn't do the job. In fact, any head that isn't in exactly the same position as the record head will induce a lack of synchronicity between sounds al-ready recorded and sounds in the process of being recorded. The only solution is to use the record head for listening to some tracks at the same time as it's recording others. That's exactly the way multi-track decks work.

Monitor Switches. In decks that allow you to overdub, there are two sets of monitor switches (although they may be hidden from the user's view and activated automatically). One switches between "source" and "tape," the other between "normal" and "sync" (sometimes called "sel-sync"). The source position allows

you to monitor the signal from the point at which it enters the deck. This is the input signal in its un-recorded, unadulterated glory, as it's being delivered to the tape deck from the source (mixer, microphone, preamplifier, instrument, or whatev-er). The tape position lets you hear the signal after it's recorded on tape.

It can be useful to switch between source and tape in order to compare what's going into the deck with what's actually getting onto the tape, but the bulk of your listening should be from the tape position. This is the safest way to record, since you will al-ways know what's on tape, which af-ter all is the crucial thing.

But if you're listening to "tape," what head is the tape being moni-tored from? This is where the "nor-mal" and "sync" switch positions come in. Normal is monitoring from the playback head. Sync is monitor-ing from the record head. It's as sim-ple as that.

While you're overdubbing, you should be listening to your tracks in the sync position. Once again, you can monitor the input either from source or tape/sync, but the latter is safest. Since the record head is designed primarily for recording rather than playback, it's generally true that it won't sound as good as the playback head. (Check this out on your deck—you'll probably hear more noise and worse frequency response when you're monitoring from the record head.) This is okay, since under conventional circumstances the only reason to monitor from the record head is as a reference while you're overdubbing. When it's time to mix, make sure all of your tracks are in normal mode, so they'll sound their best for the big playback.

Creative Applications. As with every aspect of recording technology, you can use the delay between the record and playback heads as a creative tool. In fact, doing so has been standard procedure ever since the late '50s, when Sun Records featured a jarring stutter effect on Jerry Lee Lewis' voice or Carl Perkins' guitar, and often on the entire mix.

Sun's engineers took advantage of the distinctive "slapback" delay that you get when you simultaneously monitor the same signal from both the record head (or the source) and the playback head while the tape is moving at 7.5 ips. A spare tape deck, or even a spare track of tape, can be pressed into service as a delay line—a short delay at fast tape speeds, longer at lower speeds.

How to do these things? Try to figure it out for yourself. (Check out the chapters on signal routing for a few clues.) If you think about it for 15 minutes and still find yourself scratching your head, take a look at Fig. 2-16 and Fig. 2-17. Then give it a try with your own setup.

Fig. 2-16. Tape delay using two decks: Deck 1 records while deck 2 plays back. Both decks must be operating at the same speed. The tape speed and the distance between them determine the delay time.

Fig. 2-17. Tape delay using one deck: With the deck in record, monitor from the playback head (the monitor switch's "tape" position). The delay time depends on the distance between the deck's record and playback heads, as well as tape speed.

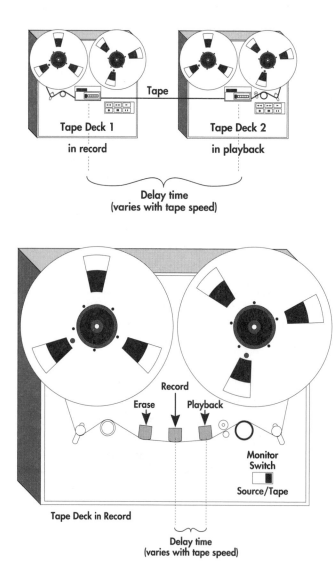

Tape

Tape Deck 1
in record

Tape Deck 2
in playback

Delay time
(varies with tape speed)

Erase   Record   Playback

Monitor
Switch

Source/Tape

Tape Deck in Record

Delay time
(varies with tape speed)

Feeling at Home in the Digital Domain

➤ It wasn't so long ago that digital recording was the new frontier of music production. Today, of course, the semi-pro market—never mind the pros—is flooded with digital signal processors, digital sampling keyboards, even all-digital mixing boards and computer-based audio workstations. Relatively affordable digital replacements for analog 2-track have been available since fairly early in the game, including Sony's digital encoders and various video decks with built-in digital audio. The latest revolutionary development is DAT (digital audio tape), and newer formats are already becoming available—don't tell your Congressman. No doubt about it, digital is more affordable, higher-fi, and easier to use than ever.

Given that you're likely to wake up one morning in the near future to find a direct-to-hard-disk turnkey digital audio workstation staring you in the face—trust me, it's bound to happen sooner or later—let's explore the principles and technology behind digital audio. This discussion builds on concepts discussed in the chapters on analog recording, so take a look at them now if you haven't already.

The Digital Difference. Sound consists of continuous variations in air pressure, which the ears translate into amplitude (loudness) and timbre (tone color, an aspect of frequency components). The key word is "continuous." Analog audio systems record and reproduce these continuities in a manner *analogous* to the original sonic pattern. Digital audio systems break up the continuity into a series of discrete values called *samples*. (In common musicianly parlance, a sample is an entire sound event. Technically speaking, though, your average "sample" consists of tens of thousands of individual samples. For the sake of clarity, we'll refer to individual samples as *sample points*.)

Here's how it works (see Fig. 2-18):

1. A sound, picked up by a microphone, is converted into a continuously varying voltage.

2. At the input of a digital audio device, the mike's output passes through an analog-to-digital (A-to-D) converter, which samples the voltage level at regular intervals.

3. The individual sample points are stored as binary numbers (computer data), either in random-access or disk memory, or on specially formulated tape.

4. Once the sound is in numerical form, it can be transformed mathematically to change its pitch, give it a reverberant quality, repeat it, and so forth—this is how digital effects units work.

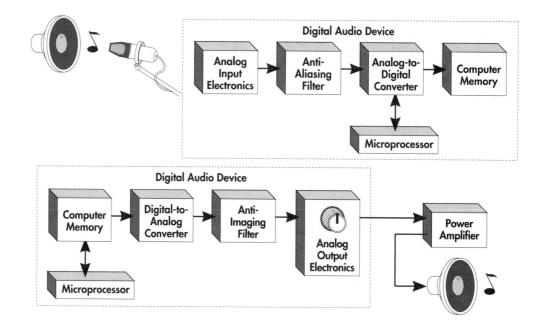

Fig. 2-18. Digital recording: Sound picked up by a microphone leaves the mike in analog form. At the input to a digital audio device, it may pass through an analog preamplifier on its way to the anti-aliasing filter, and then the analog-to-digital (A-to-D) converter. Having been transformed into a string of binary codes, the sound is stored in computer memory and/or processed mathematically. For playback, it is passed through a digital-to-analog (D-to-A) converter, an anti-imaging filter, and possibly a final analog gain stage. Now back in the analog domain, the sound is ready to be routed to an amplifier and/or other analog devices.

5. When it's time for playback, a digital-to-analog (D-to-A) converter retrieves the stored numbers and spits them out at regular intervals, converting the stream of numbers back into continuous analog voltages that can be routed to an amplifier.

Rates and Resolutions. Basically, there are only two major variables in a digital recording system, *sampling rate* and *bit resolution*. The time interval at which incoming voltages are sampled, expressed as a number of sample points per second, is the sampling rate. (The time interval at which sampled voltages are played back—generally the same as the sampling rate—is called the *sample playback rate*.) For instance, the audio encoded into a compact disc is sampled once every 1/44,100th of a second (sampling rate: 44.1kHz).

The mathematics of sampling dictate that a digital system can accurately record and reproduce frequency components only up to half of the sampling rate. Thus, the practical bandwidth (known as the *Nyquist Limit*) of a CD is 22.05kHz—plenty high, considering that most people's ears can only hear frequencies up to about 20kHz. Some high-end sampling instruments provide sampling rates of 100kHz or more. This is because recorded sounds played back from a keyboard may be transposed into a lower register, bringing down into the audio range ultrasonic frequency components that no one besides your dog has any right to hear.

Bit resolution is the number of *bits* (*b*inary dig*its*) used to define each sampled voltage. Think of it this way: You can represent the range of values between 1 and 1,000 by counting in ones or hundreds. But which method is going to be the most accurate under most circumstances? Using ones, there are 999 possible values to choose from, so a value of 177.63 can be rounded to 178. Counting by 100s, the best choice for representing 177.63 is 200. Counting by ones offers higher resolution, and thus greater accuracy.

Just as the sampling rate determines how a system handles frequency components, the bit resolution determines the fineness of the system's reproduction of amplitude. Low-resolution systems (say, 8 bits or less) tend to sound "grainy." High-res systems (16 bits or more) often sound more natural.

Flawed Perfection. Digitally recorded sound is often advertised as being "perfect." However, like analog recording, the process of digitizing sound introduces characteristic distortions (even aside from the low amplitude resolution and narrow bandwidth of low-quality digital systems).

Sampling, by its very nature, creates spurious frequency components, specifically the sum of and difference between the sampling rate and the frequency components of the sound being sampled. In a well-designed digital system, these are kept away from your ears by a pair of filters, called *anti-aliasing* and *anti-imaging* filters, that guard the system's input and output stages. In addition, there are analog components at the input and output—adjuncts to the A-to-D and D-to-A converters—that can influence a digital system's overall sound.

Ultimately, the choice to go digital in a home studio involves undeniable benefits and very slight compromises. There seems to be general agreement that most digital systems sound better than most analog systems. The lack of background noise and wide dynamic range of a good digital recording are usually enough to convince even the most skeptical ears.

The digital difference, however, means that noise and distortion must be kept under even tighter control, since there's no tape hiss to mask other problems. If you mix down to a reel-to-reel format, you're probably accustomed to the contribution tape saturation makes to the overall sound of your productions. The signal overload that produces such a sweet sound on analog tape is deadly to digital. Finally, it takes a lot more than a razor blade to edit a digital recording. The flexibility of being able to lose a chorus, repeat a verse, tight-time the dead space between songs, and so forth costs a bundle in the digital domain.

Playing the Stereo Field

➤ It wasn't so many years ago that Phil Spector, the prototypical *auteur* producer, was running around with a "Back To Mono" button pinned to his lapel. He made his biggest records—sonically as well as commercially—during the late '50s, before stereo recordings were made for the mass market.

When stereo records hit the marketplace a few years later, it took a lot of experimentation before recording engineers arrived at a conventional way of dealing with it. (Check out the early-to-midperiod Beatles records—vocals and guitars on one side, drums and bass on the other. For better or worse, you won't often find that kind of approach in the past decade.)

Today, stereo is so entrenched that you'd be hard-pressed to find an electronic audio device that doesn't include dual outputs intended to be panned hard-right and -left. With all due respect to Mr. Spector, stereo is one of the most powerful tools in the producer's arsenal, and anyone making recordings would do well to learn how to use it effectively.

Stereo Theory. Just what is stereo? Simply, the use of two independent audio channels that are routed to a pair of speakers situated to the right and left of the listener, corresponding to his two ears.

The original idea was to reproduce the sonic characteristics of the three-dimensional space in which the recorded performance originally took place. With the advent of multitracking and anechoic (nonreverberant, or "dry") recording environments, stereo became a means of creating the impression of a three-dimensional performance space where none had existed. (In fact, stereo is only two-dimensional—the dimension of height is missing—but this third dimension doesn't seem to be relevant to musical enjoyment.)

In modern times, roughly starting with the Beatles' *Sgt. Pepper's Lonely Hearts Club Band* album, sonic realism is rarely the goal. Rather, stereo is used to create fantastical sonic imagery in which performance spaces are juxtaposed, fragmented, altered, and otherwise mangled to the degree that the concept of a simulated performance space is no longer really operative.

Amazingly, the simple idea of putting one sound to the right and another to the left works like a charm. Stereo sounds bigger, brighter, fuller, more interesting—if not always more "realistic"—than mono. The slightest hint of stereo can bring an otherwise monaural recording to shimmering life. It may be a low-level slap-back echo panned to one side, a single instrument panned off-center, different colors of reverb panned hard-right and -left, different EQ settings on either side, just about anything at all. In a home-studio situation, it often makes sense to bounce your tracks to mono in order to squeeze more layers out of your 4- or 8-track setup, but be sure to slip a taste of stereo into the final mix. It can make a world of difference.

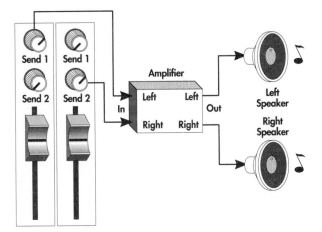

Fig. 2-19. A mono mixer can be used to create stereo mixes if it has two effect sends. The sends simply become the right and left output channels.

Stereo Practice. Since musicians traditionally perform in a right-to-left line in front of the listener, right and left speakers can be used to simulate their individual positions. As you're probably aware, you can set the precise right-to-left position of each instrument by twisting the pan knob on each of your (stereo) mixer's input channels.

What's actually happening is this: When the knob is fully to the right, the signal is sent to the right side at full level. If you turn the knob a little to the left, less level is sent to the right and a small amount is routed to the left—that is, the musician appears to have taken a few steps to the left. At the center position, the knob sends equal amounts (half of the full level) to each side, which gives the impression that the sound is coming from between the two speakers. It's as though you were moving two faders or effect sends, one for the right and one for the left, in contrary motion. In fact, if you have a mono board with two effect sends, you can use the effect sends to create stereo mixes (see Fig. 2-19).

Stereo Ambience. The back-to-front aspect of the sonic space is taken care of by reverberation, which simulates the complex and subtle web of echoes that spread throughout a room whenever a sound occurs. The greater the ratio of reverberation to dry signal, the farther away the sound appears to originate. However, since sound waves tend to bounce a bit unevenly on either side of the room, reverb should be in stereo, as well—that is, slightly different on either side. Even if you're working with something as monaural as a solo acoustic guitar sitting dead-center, a little stereo reverb makes a huge difference.

These days, most reverb devices have stereo outputs that send out compatible right and left signals. Pan them hard-right and -left, and you'll get convincing audio reflections. If you happen to have only a couple of outmoded mono spring reverbs—which can be bought for a song these days, by the way—pan them to the right and left and feed

Fig. 2-20. Make-do stereo ambience with a microphone and two mixer channels (EQ optional): The mike, located in a room other than your control room and positioned to hear room reflections, picks up the mono mix coming from the speaker. The instrument channels and the mike output are mixed together, each with a different pan position. EQing the mike signal allows you to fine-tune the effect.

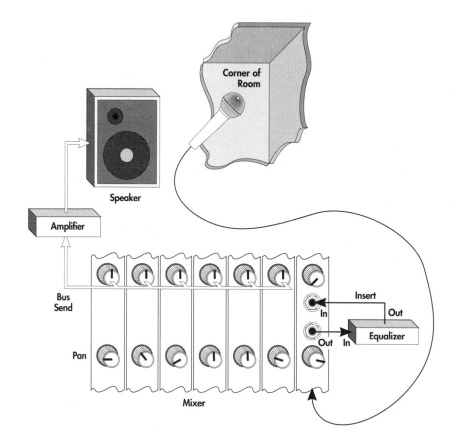

them from the same bus (a Y-cable will do the trick). Then EQ their returns until they sound as similar as possible. If you have only one mono reverb, split its output to a quick delay and pan the original and delayed versions opposite, or split it to two EQ units set differently and panned to either side.

Okay. What if you don't have any reverb at all? Set up a quick delay and give it enough regeneration (feedback) to produce a reverbish tail. Pan it about 20% off-center and send just about everything through it in very small amounts. It's not the greatest, but it helps.

Now we're down to the dregs. You don't even have a delay unit or, for that matter, a spare tape deck with

which to produce old-fashioned tape delay. But if you have a microphone, you can play your (rather dry) mono mix through a speaker (located in a room other than your control room), place the mike on the other side of the room pointed at a ceiling corner, and mix the mike's output with the original mix, panning them somewhat apart (see Fig. 2-20). If you give this a shot, try to free up an EQ unit for the mike signal. Some severe tweaking may be required to make the most of the effect.

Advanced Stereo. You can pick up a number of great stereo techniques by listening carefully to pop records, where they're rampant. You'll hear oppositely panned double-tracked vocals, long and short delays off to one side, right/left splits of flanged and straight signals, hi-hats panning back and forth, and on and on.

But to get back to those old Beatles records: Why *not* put the bass and drums on one side? Well, there are reasons. For one thing, placing such prominent elements off to one side makes it harder for a listener to hear a decent balance if he's not directly between the speakers. Also, scientifically speaking, human ears aren't very good at discriminating the directionality of low frequencies, so placing a bass guitar to one side may be less effective than putting a higher-frequency sound in its place.

Still, where music is concerned, it seems a shame to eliminate any of the possibilities. If you think it sounds good to put everything but the reverb returns off to one side, then do it. Your friends may call you a lunatic, but you can always come back by insisting that it's a stroke of genius.

No Noise is Good Noise

➤ In the studio, the two nasties—after bad music and bad performances—are distortion and noise. In a budget studio, it's more or less impossible to reduce them to the levels found in a well-designed professional environment. However, with a little care, it's not difficult to keep them under control.

Know Your Enemy. Basically, noise is the stuff that sounds like *shhh* or *ssss,* and distortion is any other difference between the signal you want to record and the same signal as it comes back from tape. (AC hum, which is leakage from the power source into the audio line, is another beast entirely.)

Technically, noise and distortion can't be separated. In spec measurements, they're often designated THD+n, or "total harmonic distortion plus noise." Even this label is misleading, though, since *harmonic* distortion and *inharmonic* distortion—which may or may not be noise—are also inseparable. Another common spec is S/N, or "signal-to-noise ratio." This refers to the difference between the loudest signal a unit can generate before distortion sets in and the residual noise level when the unit is silent.

Harmonic distortion adds frequencies harmonically related to the original signal. It tends to blend into the music, so it's relatively benign. Standard guitar-type distortion—also known as *clipping*—is harmonic, often rich in "smooth" even-order harmonics, rather than "harsh" odd-order harmonics. That's one reason why it sounds good. The lesson here is that sometimes distortion can be desirable. Inharmonic distortion components aren't harmonically related, so they strike the ear as more annoying. Noise is also inharmonic, but consists of energy more or less evenly distributed across a band of the frequency spectrum, rather than a set of discrete frequencies. (Harmonic distortion, inharmonic distortion, and noise are frequency-related distortions. Oddly, distortions in the amplitude domain such as compression are almost never considered under the heading "distortion.")

Causes. Undue distortion occurs anytime the signal level exceeds the tolerance of a given component in your recording system. Undue noise is likely to occur when the signal level is lower than the level at which a given component is designed to perform optimally. The difference between a device's optimal level, which you can think of as 0dB, and the level at which distortion occurs, which is some number of dB higher, is called *headroom*. In this range, you'll get the least noise and the least distortion.

The available headroom is bound to be slightly different in your amplifier, microphone, mixer, the mixer's on-board EQ, the tape deck's heads, the tape itself, and so on, so you can see that keeping the signal at the best level for every piece of gear in your studio is a tall order. Fortunately, industry-wide level standards make it likely that most devices will work together fairly well without too much attention.

Coping. Most studio components have LED meters or indicators to give you some idea of their headroom. LEDs are useful for judging the input setting at which a given device is seeing 0dB, but distortion often occurs well above or below the clipping level indicated on the meter.

If quick-and-dirty is good enough for your purposes (or if your ears tell you that everything sounds great), you can rely on meters completely. The more rigorous way of doing things involves using a 1kHz test tone to find a nominal 0dB input level setting for each device in your studio, and then adjusting various outputs so that they're not sending out too much more than that. This can be an involved procedure; rather than go into it here, we'll take a look at some other ways to keep noise and distortion out of your recordings.

• Keep levels as high as possible (short of audible distortion). This doesn't apply to the individual instruments in a mix, of course, since in that situation levels should be determined by the demands of the music. In virtually all other cases, hotter is better. This is particularly true of levels you send to tape during tracking or mixdown, because analog tape is often a primary source of noise, and because—depending on the quality of the tape and your tape deck's heads—tape can usually handle levels much higher than 0dB.

• Keep cable runs as short as possible. A signal degrades as it travels through a wire, so the more direct the route, the better. If long runs are necessary, use high-quality ("low-loss, low-capacitance") cable.

• Likewise, keep signal chains as short and simple as possible. Every electronic component you send a signal through degrades it a bit. Often, recording is a compromise between achieving the desired effect and keeping the sound pristine. Your best option may well be an uncomplicated, dry, straight-ahead mix.

• Tape speed also has an effect on residual noise. Higher speed makes for a higher-resolution recording. There's more tape surface to capture fluctuations in signal voltage, and thus a better signal-to-noise ratio. If you can afford the extra tape, use the highest speed your deck allows.

• When you're mixing, be aware of instruments that don't play all the time. Whenever an instrument is silent, pull down its fader or mute its channel. (Be sure to bring it back in time for the instrument to re-enter!) A noise gate can perform the same function automatically, but cheap gates sometimes add nearly as much noise as they eliminate. Listen before you buy.

• If the noise coming from a given instrument or tape track is out of hand, try rolling off some of the highs using an equalizer. If this interferes too much with the sound of the instrument itself, try to locate a band in which the noise is prominent in a lower frequency range, and cut back on that instead.

• These days it's not uncommon, even in home studios, to reduce noise and distortion by mixing to a digital 2-track format. DAT (digital audio tape) is the most convenient one, but there are others. These include VCR machines with digital audio tracks and digital encoders such as the old Sony PCM-501. Computer-based digital audio recording/editing systems such as Digidesign's Sound-Tools (for the Macintosh), Hybrid Arts' ADAP (for the Atari ST), and the system made by Spectral Synthesis (for the IBM) offer a more powerful, if more expensive, alternative.

• Electrical balancing can lower a studio's noise floor by several dB. Balanced lines use a slick phase-reversal technique in order to remove all of the noise that accumulates in the wire due to radio-frequency (RF) interference and power-line leakage. Professional equipment often comes with balanced inputs and outputs (usually associated with 3-pin XLR connectors), while semi-pro gear is almost always unbalanced (using RCA or 1/4" connectors). A good technician can convert any system from unbalanced to balanced, but it's not an inexpensive proposition. It's probably best to hold back on this until your studio is generating substantial income.

• And then there's noise reduction. Noise reduction systems come in two flavors: *double-ended* and *single-ended*. Double-ended systems such as Dolby and dbx are intended to reduce tape noise, and are generally more effective. They involve both an encoding process (when the tape is recorded) and a decoding process (when the tape is played back), and don't do the trick unless both processes are employed. Encoding without decoding, or vice-versa, simply distorts the signal. With a single-ended system, you simply route the noisy signal through the unit, which filters out some of the noise (and often most of the high frequencies as well). The Rocktron Hush II and the Symetrix 511 are effective, affordable single-ended systems.

Mixed Media: A Survey of Recording Formats

➤ Recording media—the materials that your music can be recorded on—come in a number of shapes and sizes, better known to the audio world as *formats*. Each offers compromises among cost, convenience, capability, and basic technology involved.

The two basic divisions are digital and analog. If you're like most people, you still live in the analog world. You probably use cassette (stereo, 4-track, or both) and analog 1/4" formats most often. Still, there are other options, and you may need to be familiar with them from time to time. This may happen when you add a few tracks to a friend's production, bring your home tapes into a professional studio for a makeover, or simply want to upgrade your studio's capabilities. It's good to have a little background when the time comes for you to know whether your quarter-track stereo tape will play back on somebody else's 4- or 8-track machine.

To that end, here's a quick-and-dirty rundown of the various formats you're likely to run into.

Analog Tape. Analog tape is by far the most common basic medium, but probably not for long. As computer technology becomes more sophisticated and less expensive, we can expect to see the end of tape recording for many applications. Until then, you can take some satisfaction in knowing that analog is still generally simpler to use, more flexible, and less prone to failure than digital.

The variables in tape formats revolve around tape width, tape speed, the number of discrete electromagnetic fields (tracks) distributed across the tape's width, and whether the tape is intended to play back in two directions or only one.

Tape Width. Cassette tape is 1/8" wide. Open-reel tape comes in 1/4", 1/2", 1", and 2" sizes. Widths larger than 1/4" are generally associated with professional formats, while cassettes and 1/4" reels are used at home.

Tape Speed. Cassettes usually run at 1-7/8 ips (inches per second). Some professional 2-track machines and most 4-track cassette decks aspire to higher quality by running twice as fast. Open-reel 1/4" machines usually begin at 7-1/2 ips, and increase from there; 1/2" and 1" formats begin at 15 ips, while 2" tape seldom runs at less than 30 ips. The current standard for professional applications in all widths (except cassettes) is 30 ips.

Number of Tracks. These days, you can find cassette machines that pack an incredible eight tracks into the 1/8" tape width, although 2- and 4-track cassettes are far more common. Tape in 1/4" width also varies between two and eight tracks, while 1/2" formats vary between two and sixteen tracks (2-track 1/2" is the most popular analog format for professional mixdowns). The 1" format was invented for 8-track recording, and expanded to 16 tracks; modern 2" tape always holds 24 tracks (although some 2" 16-track machines were commonly used in the '70s).

Two Playback Directions or One? This is really only an issue in 2- and 4-track formats. Look at it this way: A 4-track cassette deck records four tracks across the tape's width and is capable of playing them all back at once. On the other hand, a stereo cassette deck records four tracks as well, but plays back only two tracks (stereo) at a time. You have to turn the tape over to hear the other two.

This distinction gives rise to a few terms describing the number of tracks on tape independently of whether the format is intended for stereo or multi-track. These are: *full-track, half-track,* and *quarter-track.* They simply refer to the number of electromagnetic divisions (tracks) across the tape's width.

Full-track means no divisions—the entire surface of the tape is encoded with one signal (see Fig. 2-21). This can only be a mono format, and it can only play in one direction. If you turn it over to hear "Side 2," you'll hear Side 1 playing backward. Half-track means two divisions (see Fig. 2-22). It can either be stereo in one direction ("half-track stereo") or mono in two directions ("half-track mono"). Quarter-track formats encode four tracks across the tape's width (see Fig. 2-23). This yields the usual stereo arrangement (two tracks in each of two directions, or "quarter-track stereo") and the usual 4-track format (four tracks in one direction).

If quadrophonic sound hadn't died in the mid '70s, we might have an "eighth-track" format that played four tracks in each of two directions. As it is, this kind of terminology stops after four tracks; any more tracks always indicates a multi-track arrangement with playback in only one direction.

Digital Tape. Most of the distinctions between digital tape formats (AES/EBU, DASH, etc.) have to do with the various mathematical processes by which sound is encoded and decoded. These distinctions are critical in professional applications such as CD mastering and digital transfers. In a home situation, however, they're not likely to arise, and

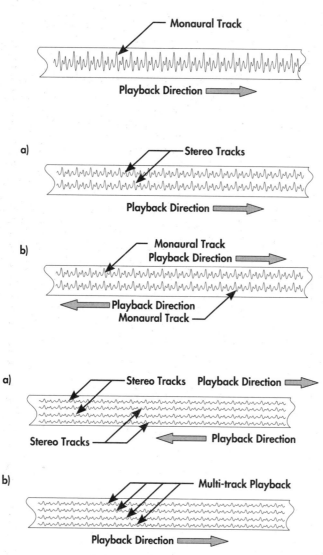

Fig. 2-21. A full-track tape has only one mono track. It can only be played in one direction.

Fig. 2-22. Half-track stereo tapes play back in stereo in only one direction (a), while half-track mono tapes play back in mono in two directions (b).

Fig. 2-23. Stereo cassettes use a quarter-track arrangement. The tape plays back two tracks of stereo in each direction (a). A 4-track cassette, on the other hand, offers multi-track playback in only one direction (b).

principle as video technology, and is thus fundamentally different from conventional analog recording formats.

All DAT tapes have the same width, run at the same speed, and are designed to encode audio in 16 bits of data. However, the music on a DAT tape may be recorded at a variety of sampling rates, usually 44.1kHz or 48kHz. Tapes recorded at one sampling rate will not play back on machines designed to play back at a different rate, so if you're taking a DAT tape from one studio to another, make sure the same sampling rate is available at both locations.

Two other digital tape formats, holdovers from the pre-DAT days, are found in home recording setups. Audio can be digitized by a stand-alone digital converter and recorded on a standard consumer-grade video deck, either VHS or Beta. In this case, both the converter unit and the video deck are required for recording and playback. In addition, some video decks feature digital audio onboard, which requires no external encoding or decoding. These video decks simply offer digital audio as an alternative to the usual analog audio tracks.

Tapeless Digital Formats. Far from being part of some scenario depicting the future of home recording, tapeless recording is here, now. The technology is still in its infancy, but

in any case will probably change before any of us have enough money to invest in them.

Most practical for home studios is that wonder of modern technology, DAT (Digital Audio Tape). The basic fact of DAT—and all well-designed digital formats—is that the tape itself adds virtually no hiss to your music. DAT tape is housed in a shell somewhat smaller than a cassette and similar in design to a VHS video tape. In fact, it uses the same rotating-head it's not too soon to hop on the bus. A number of personal computer-based digital audio systems are in their third or fourth revision, including Digidesign's products for the Macintosh, Hybrid Arts' for the Atari ST, and Spectral Synthesis' for the IBM. A very low-cost alternative is Macromind's MacRecorder in conjunction with Passport's AudioTrax software for the Mac. These systems record digital audio directly to the computer's hard disk drive. Be prepared to spend a bit of extra time and money for the privilege of standing on the cutting edge, but the rewards may well be worth it.

In fact, many home-studio owners can experiment with aspects of tapeless recording with a piece of equipment they may already own: a digital sampler. The medium here is RAM (computer memory) and/or floppy disks. Sixteen-bit samplers that offer rates of 44.1kHz and up have the potential to record and play back CD-quality digital audio. Lesser bit resolutions and sampling rates can also yield good results.

The amounts of sampling time available may be limited to 30 seconds or less, but with a little innovative spirit you might find it possible to repeat a couple of short segments to form a longer basic track. When you take on an assignment like that, your own creative energy blasts you out of the format wars and back into the world of music. Which is where you really belong.

The Recording Engineer's Palette: Equipment and Techniques

The Studio's Ears: Microphone Technology

➤ Microphones are the ears of the studio. In fact, they use a technology very similar to the human eardrum: a membrane that gets pushed back and forth by the compressions and rarefactions of air that constitute sound. Another way to look at microphones is to consider them inverted speakers. Speakers translate (or, in scientific parlance, *transduce*) fluctuations in electrical voltage into vibrations of air molecules via a moving membrane (the cone). Likewise, microphones translate motion in the air into electromagnetic fluctuations via a similar, but much lighter and more sensitive, membrane (the diaphragm).

The diaphragm is attached to a magnet that moves, in turn, back and forth between the two poles of an electromagnet, creating a disturbance in the magnetic field. Because the electrical forces involved are very small and the diaphragm itself is also small, the electrical current created is very weak. This explains the low signal levels associated with microphones; "mike level" is a great deal lower than "line level."

Technologically, mikes are distinguished by three factors: pickup pattern, transducer design, and impedance.

Pickup Pattern. Any mike should pick up your voice loud and clear if you're speaking directly in front of it. But what if you're in back of it? Or off to one side? It depends on the mike's *pickup pattern*. The pattern describes how efficiently the microphone picks up sounds coming from various directions. Many high-end mikes are capable of switching among two or three pickup patterns, but most offer only one.

The most basic pattern is called *omnidirectional,* or omni (see Fig. 3-1a). As the name suggests, an omni mike picks up sounds equally regardless of where they originate with respect to the front, sides, or rear of the mike's capsule. This might be great for a monaural recording of a solo acoustic guitar or an a cappella group, but clearly this kind of pattern isn't the most sensible if there's anything else going on in the room that you don't want the mike to pick up (say, a vocalist), or if you want to create a stereo image. Mikes with the omni pattern tend to have the best frequency response, so they are used occasionally in a studio situation, but their applications are limited.

The *cardioid pattern* (see Fig. 3-1b) is the most generally useful. It provides maximum sensitivity directly in front of the mike, with decreasing sensitivity to either side and a dead

Fig. 3-1. Microphone pickup patterns: omnidirectional (a), cardioid (b), and figure-8 (c).

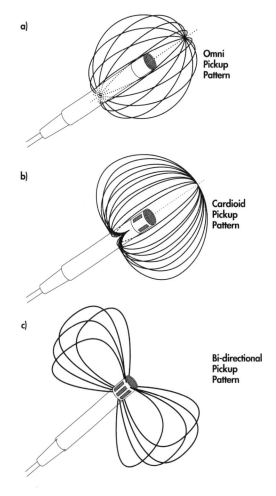

a) Omni Pickup Pattern

b) Cardioid Pickup Pattern

c) Bi-directional Pickup Pattern

noise outside of your living room window.

Unless you spend a lot of time in a studio, you aren't likely to encounter the *bi-directional,* or figure-8, pickup pattern (see Fig. 3-1c). This pattern is most sensitive at points directly in front and in back of the capsule. The applications: A mono track of two vocalists who are facing one another, or two side-by-side tom toms. Another useful technique is to use the rear face to pick up room ambience, while the front face listens to a vocalist or instrumentalist during overdubbing. Of course, you could use two cardioid mikes for any of these situations and maintain separation for mixing or further overdubbing.

Transducer Design. The two most common transducer designs are *dynamic* and *condenser.* A third major design is the *ribbon* mike, but since these are rare, fragile, and very expensive, there's no compelling reason to deal with them here. (The PZM, or *pressure zone microphone—* also known as a boundary microphone—is another option, but it's not very common. A PZM's body is a flat metal plate, which is mounted directly on a wall or other flat surface. The idea is to eliminate phase problems by picking up only direct sound waves, and no reflections. Check out Radio Shack's legendary bargain PZM if you're interested in experimenting.)

Dynamic mikes use a coil of wire mounted on the diaphragm to generate their signals. When the diaphragm moves, the coil moves as

spot directly in back. If you map out the sensitivity around the capsule of a cardioid mike, you end up with a shape something like that of a heart, with the point of the heart extending out in front of the mike and the heart's cleft directly in back. This heart shape is where the name cardioid comes from.

Since the cardioid pattern tends to block sounds emanating from behind the mike, it can be good for recording multiple instruments in the same room while maintaining some degree of separation between them. It also tends to block the sound of your tape deck if it's in the same room, or street well, vibrating within a magnetic field. This creates the kind of electro-magnetic fluctuations your tape deck likes to see.

Dynamic mikes tend to be inexpensive, shock-resistant, and difficult to distort even at excessively high volumes. Their ruggedness makes them safe to carry around, and their tolerance for loud sources makes them the choice for placing in front of a kick drum or a Marshall stack.

The trade-off is in the sensitivity of the diaphragm, which translates into less-than-ideal high-frequency and transient responses. Ideally, recording an acoustic guitar requires excellent high-frequency and transient responses, while these factors are less critical for, say, vocals. That doesn't mean you should give up on dynamic mikes, though. Just be sure to compare specs, and, above all, listen. It may be that a low-cost dynamic is perfect for your needs.

Rather than a wire coil and a magnet, a condenser mike uses two tiny electrically charged plates, one of which is the diaphragm. When the diaphragm moves in response to a sound, the distance between the plates fluctuates, resulting in a fluctuating voltage, and voila—you get an electrical signal analogous to the sound, ripe and ready for recording.

In order to charge the plates, and to boost the very low signal this system generates, condenser mikes require a power supply. When it's external to the mike, the power supply is known as *phantom power*. Phantom power may be built into a mixing console (very unusual to find

in a home situation) or is available from a box provided by the mike's manufacturer. Some condenser mikes use internal batteries rather than phantom power.

Condensers offer the high-end and transient response that dynamic mikes tend to be weak in, but their enhanced sensitivity means that they're more fragile. They won't stand for as much rock-and-roll abuse, such as rough handling and excessive volume. Until recently, they were also much more expensive, but these days a number of companies offer relatively low-cost condenser mikes perfectly suited to home-studio use.

Impedance. *Impedance* refers to a circuit's tendency to resist the flow of electrons through the wire. (Another form of this phenomenon is known as resistance.) There are only two standard impedance levels for microphones: high and low. Low-impedance (or *low*-Z) mikes are generally of higher quality. In addition, they are electrically balanced, which results in lower noise and consistent performance when cable runs exceed about 20'. You can tell a low-impedance mike by the 3-pin XLR plug that connects it to a cable.

On the other hand, high-Z mikes come with 1/4" connectors, and are electrically unbalanced. They're generally less expensive, but you get what you pay for.

What if you want to use a low-Z mike, but your mixer or tape deck doesn't provide a three-pin jack? In this case you need an *impedance-matching transformer,* available from electronics and pro-audio supply stores. This does the proper impedance transformation, as well as the un-balancing act, necessary to get low-Z mikes into 1/4" inputs.

Choosing a Microphone. The recording engineer's job is less science and more art than the title would suggest. In choosing the proper microphone for a given recording task, the basic aim is to use an accurate, sensitive, generally hi-fi mike. After that, the decision is as much aesthetic and stylistic as technical. For a vocalist with a Rod Stewart rasp, one engineer might choose a particularly bright mike. Another might have a similar aural concept but use his old standby vocal mike, sweetening it with some top-end EQ, while a third might choose to de-emphasize the raspiness by using a duller mike.

High-quality pro studios keep a variety of mikes on hand so that engineers can exercise their artistry. At home, though, having a selection of top-quality mikes isn't so practical. For one thing, the funds probably aren't available. Furthermore, frequency characteristics, transient response, and noise level of a home studio may not do justice to a fancy microphone, and between ranch-style room acoustics and signal-routing and -processing limitations, you may not have enough control over other signals to create the ideal context for a particular mike's sound.

For a home studio, the priorities should include value, accuracy, sensi-

tivity, and durability. Stick with low-impedance for low noise and good sound. If you're a stay-at-home type with a little extra cash, and you manage to get the sounds you need without resorting to high volume, look into a condenser. If you travel, or if the only way to get the guitar sound you want is to slam a mike in front of a Marshall set to 11, or if you have to mike drums, a dynamic might be best for you. Pignose-style practice amps, which produce great over-driven sounds without the high volume and bulk of, say, a Marshall stack, make it relatively easy to record rock and roll guitar in your living room without disturbing the neighbors by shoving just about any old mike an inch or two from the speaker.

As with other audio products, you get what you pay for. Spending a few extra clams on a sensitive, accurate mike can make a big difference in your sound. The market offers enough variety, though, that it's not too hard to balance cost against other factors. If you can spend the money, consider buying two identical mikes. This gives you the option of stereo miking for acoustic instruments, ambience, and various experiments. You can also mike more than one source simultaneously while maintaining separation. If you have overdubbing capability, it certainly isn't necessary to own more than one mike, but it's nice if you can spring for it.

The Anatomy of a Mixer

> **Demystifying the Mixing Console.** To the uninitiated, a professional mixing console is a bewildering array of sliders, knobs, buttons, meters, and LEDs. Even a small semi-pro board can look pretty imposing if you're not familiar with the general nature of the beast. Either way, it can be enlightening to consider the mixer as a simple grid of inputs and outputs (see Fig 3-2).

According to this scheme, inputs are represented vertically, outputs horizontally. Thus, the mixer's input channels appear in the diagram as vertical lines. Although they look very different on the console's panel, they look

bus returns (effect returns, tape returns, etc.) are actually stripped-down input channels, so they appear as vertical lines, too. The master stereo outputs run horizontally. The various bus sends—effect, aux(iliary), cue, and tape—are output buses, too; they also appear as horizontal lines.

Wherever an input line intersects with an output line, there's usually an opportunity to feed some of the (vertical) signal into the (horizontal) output bus, mixing it with whatever signal is already flowing through that bus. This is indicated by a dot at the intersection. This grid scheme works for any mixer, from the top-of-the-

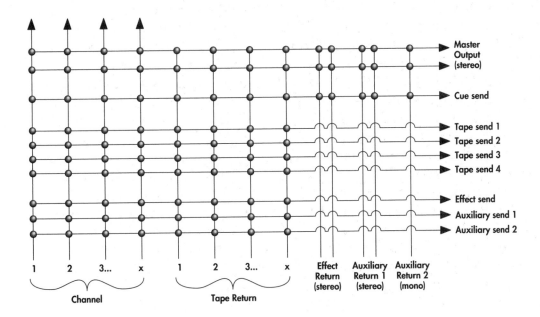

Fig. 3-2. Any mixer can be represented as a grid of inputs and outputs. Inputs (including returns) are shown as vertical. Outputs (including sends) are the horizontal lines. Intersections at which mixing takes place are indicated by dots.

line SSL console to the most inexpensive Boss unit.

To further demystify the mixing console, I'll risk stating the obvious and point out that a mixer comprises several more-or-less identical audio channels, laid out side by side. Each channel is, by itself, relatively simple, so the plethora of controls actually reduces to a handful of essential functions. These functions are pretty standard from mixer to mixer, and we'll cover them one by one in the next section. In order to get to them, however, a signal must enter one of the mixer's channel inputs.

Channel Inputs. Before we go any further, let's get some nomenclature straight: A mixer has *channels*. A tape deck has *tracks*. If you ever hear one of your bandmates talking about plugging the guitar into another track on the mixer, look him straight in the eye and give him a dose of the most ear-splitting feedback you can muster.

Like any input, a channel input is designed to accept a particular signal-level range, either low ("microphone-level") or high ("line-level"). In order to provide some flexibility, most mixers include both. Generally, the mike-level inputs accept a balanced 3-prong XLR plug, while line-level inputs accept a 1/4" plug. However, inputs designed for different levels may use the same jack/plug format. In this case, low-level inputs should be labelled something like "-50dBm," and high-level inputs should be marked "-20dBm," or thereabouts. (If you want to connect a 1/4" plug to an XLR jack, or vice-versa, you'll

need a *direct box,* which adapts the levels and balancing.)

Some channel inputs offer a high/low switch. Use the low-level setting for microphones, outputs from effects designed for connection to guitar amps (stomp boxes and the like), and direct outputs from electric guitars. The high-level setting is appropriate for just about everything else.

Tracking Versus Mixing. From a channel's point of view, recording basic tracks and mixing are entirely different procedures. When you're recording several simultaneous tape tracks, each channel's input is likely to be connected to a microphone (direct box, synthesizer, or whatever) which is routed in turn to a tape input via an output bus. But consider this: You don't want to be listening to signals going *to* tape. You want to hear the signals coming *from* tape, both to make sure the right signals got there and to hear them once they've been recorded.

This is a signal-routing conundrum that larger boards solve by providing each channel with a *tape return*—a spare input that makes it possible to both accept a microphone and monitor the tape deck's output using the same channel. If you're savvy with a patch bay, you can use two sets of channels, one for the input signals and one for the tape deck's outputs, and monitor only the latter set. With a smaller board, though, it's simplest to plug the microphones, instruments, and/or processor outputs directly into the tape deck, and connect its outputs to

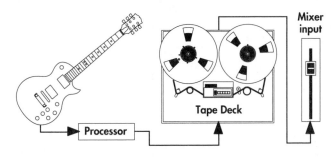

Mixer
input

Tape Deck

Processor

Fig. 3-3. The simplest way to monitor from the tape deck while recording basic tracks is to connect microphones, instruments, and/or processor outputs to the deck, and connect its outputs to the board. To monitor the input signal, switch the deck's output switch to "source." To hear what's on tape, switch it to "tape."

the board (see Fig. 3-3). That way, you can monitor through—and from—the tape deck without making any other connections. To monitor the input signal, switch the deck's output switch to "source." To hear what's on tape, switch it to "tape."

Mixing is a much less complicated situation: You simply want to hear what's coming from the tape machine. Once again, large boards make this relatively easy by providing a button that switches the channel sources from microphones to tape machine outputs *en masse*. If you're using a small board, and you've set it up as described above, you'll already be ready to mix.

How Many? How many channels should you have? It depends on the kinds of productions you tend to do, and on the signal-routing possibilities of your setup. If your studio is based on multi-track tape rather than virtual MIDI tracks, you should certainly have as many mixer inputs as tape tracks, plus two or three for good measure. (The extra inputs will come in handy for adding live guitars or vocals while mixing, patching in signal processors for which there aren't enough effect returns, and the like.) If you do a lot of live recording, then recording basic tracks will

require nine or ten mike-level inputs just for the drum mikes, plus enough for the rest of the band. A mixdown in a moderately elaborate MIDI setup may require 20 or 30 line-level inputs. And if you're into outboard effects, that only adds to the burden.

Of course, there are various ways to compromise. For instance, depending on the musical situation, you might find it possible to process your entire mix through a stereo reverb, adjusting the wet/dry mix at the reverb unit itself. This might free up the mixer's stereo effect return to be used as two additional input channels (see Fig. 3-4). Similarly, you can premix by using the mix output of your drum machine or multi-timbral synth module or sampler, rather than the individual outputs.

Functions and Features. Signal flow is the key to understanding any mixer. Signals entering the mixer get *mixed* (combined) and/or *split* (duplicated), and, in one form or another, come back out. From there, they might be recorded, amplified, processed, monitored, or dealt with in whatever way strikes your fancy.

It's not difficult to follow the signal flow from a single channel input through the modules that perform basic functions and to the various

Fig. 3-4. Extra mixer inputs: Depending on the musical situation, you can route your mixer's master output through a stereo reverb, adjusting the wet/dry mix at the reverb unit itself. This frees the mixer's stereo effect return to be used as two additional input channels.

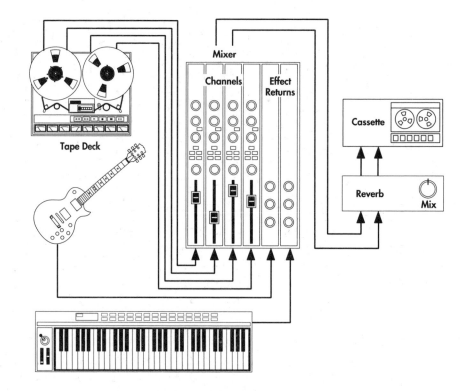

outputs. Most mixers are designed to represent this flow graphically, from the top to the bottom of each channel (with the exception of the fader—see Fig. 3-5). Generally speaking, a signal enters at a channel input and passes through a preamp, an equalizer, and a fader. Then it gets split off to signal processors and recording devices via bus sends, and to the master stereo outputs via a panning knob. From there, it may pass on to the channel's direct output.

Preamplifier. In the signal chain of your average mixer, the first stage after the input jack is a preamplifier. The potentiometer (knob, slider, or whatever) that feeds the preamp stage may be marked "sensitivity," "trim," "mic pre," or simply "mic."

The preamp serves a few purposes. Basically, it boosts low-level signals generated by microphones up to the line-level range, where the mixer can deal with them more readily. Also, it allows you to tweak any input signal up or down so that its most useful level, in terms of mixing, corresponds roughly with the channel fader's 0dB position. This way, you can place the faders for even relatively quiet sounds in the middle of their throw, giving yourself the widest range of fader motion in which to make adjustments.

The preamp's knob shouldn't be turned all the way down unless the incoming signal is very hot. The normal operating level—no boost or cut, or 0dB—is usually about one-third of the knob's throw, so that's a good starting point. You can find the exact 0dB point by sending a sine-wave test tone into the channel at its nominal level (+4dB for pro gear, -10dB for semi-pro) and turning up the preamp until you hear it distort. This will happen just above 0dB. (For more information, refer to the section on gain-staging in the section labeled "Refining Your Sound: Advanced Techniques.")

On the other hand, like any audio device, a channel's preamp will overload and clip (distort) if you feed it too high a level. It's nice to have an LED indicator that lets you know when the preamp circuit is clipping. On the other hand, you might want to overdrive the preamp intentionally in order to use it as a distortion effect.

Equalization. If EQ is built into the board, the signal passes through it next. This is where its frequency content gets carved into a viable piece of the audio jigsaw puzzle that is the final mix.

Most boards that have EQ allow you to switch it in and out so that you can hear the signal alternately affected and unaffected. If the board you're interested in doesn't let you do this, don't buy it. If the board you already own doesn't, consider having it modified. Switchable EQ may seem like a small feature to go out of your way for, but when you're searching for the right settings to fit a sound into the mix, it's crucial.

Insert. After the equalizer, and possibly at other places in the signal chain, the mixer may provide an insert point, a place of convenient access to the signal. This is simply an input/output pair (normally bridged by a jumper) where the channel's signal is available for routing elsewhere and back again. For instance, the insert point is a good place from which a lead guitar (either live or on tape) can be sent to, and returned from, a flanger, delay line, or other processor intended to affect only that signal.

Fader. The channel's signal, pumped up by the preamp and twisted out of shape by the equalizer, reaches the fader next. A fader is nothing more than a volume knob designed for grabbing on short notice. Its 0dB point is just above the middle of its throw; this is usually indicated on the fader panel as a set of colored marks or a shaded range. Why a range instead of a discrete point? The lower end of the range is the level required to achieve 0dB at the master output bus if all faders are active at once. The higher end is the level for a single fader by itself.

Incidentally, when a fader isn't in use, keep it fully down. An unnecessarily raised fader adds extra noise to your mix.

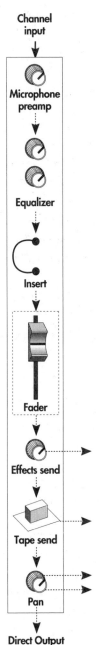

Fig. 3-5. The signal path of a typical mixer channel: The signal passes through a preamp, an equalizer, and a fader. Then it gets split off to signal processors and recording devices via bus sends, and to the master stereo outputs via a panning knob. It may pass on to a direct output.

Solo and Mute. These are very simple, but very helpful, functions. The mute switch blocks the signal from getting any farther down the chain, most notably to the final mix outputs, so that an instrument can be totally removed from the mix momentarily. The solo button is exactly the opposite: It mutes all channels except its own.

Mutes and solos make it possible to listen to individual instruments and hand-picked groups of instruments without having to change fader levels. This is important because fader positions, down to the most minute increment, can be critical to a good mix. Once the faders are on their way to being set, you don't want to mess with them if you can avoid it.

You won't find solo and mute switches on low-cost boards because the hardware is relatively expensive. This makes serious mixing in a moderately elaborate home studio a lot more arduous than it should be. Unfortunately, the only substitute for soloing is to pull down every fader except the one you're interested in, and then return them to their previous positions—an operation that, once you're well into the mixdown process, is more counterproductive than helpful. (If you're working with a MIDI sequencer, it's usually possible to solo individual virtual tracks).

However, there are a couple of ways to mute an individual channel without a mute switch *per se*. The easiest is simply to pull the plug out of the relevant input channel: *Voila!* Instant muting capability. Also, the source/tape switches on a multi-track tape deck can be used for muting.

Buses. In a mixer channel's signal chain, either before or after the fader you might have the opportunity to split the signal off to a *bus*. This is where the mixing really takes place. Each channel can contribute a controlled amount of its signal to any of a number of buses; ultimately, the buses contain a mix of several different channels, to be routed anywhere you please.

Typically, you'd route a bus output to a reverb unit (effect), the musician's headphones (cue), or one input of a multi-track tape deck. Keep in mind, though, that buses are signal-routing tools. They are designed with specific purposes in mind, but they exist to route signals wherever they need to go. Any destination is valid.

Sends. The control that feeds a bus is known as its *send*. Sends come in two basic types: switches and knobs. For instance, a mixing board designed for use with an eight-track tape deck might include, with each input channel, a group of eight buttons (often called the *multi-track bus*). Each button feeds a specific tape input; pressing one splits the channel's signal off to the corresponding tape track. To mix several channels to a single tape track, all you have to do is press the proper button on each channel.

A more common type of send is a rotary knob. The advantage here is that you can control the level you're sending—the push-button type sends all or nothing. Rotary sends are designed to route, say, a little of the vocal to the reverb, a little less of the guitar, and a whole lot of the snare drum.

Pre-Fader Versus Post-Fader. More significant, sends differ in their placement in the signal path: they are either *post-fader* or *pre-fader* (or switchable between the two). That is, they're wired before or after the fader (see Fig. 3-6).

The signal level available to a post-fader send is the level set by the fader. If the fader is low, the send can be turned all the way up and only a small amount of signal will find its way into the bus. Furthermore, the level going to a post-fader send changes as the fader moves up and down. Most sends labelled "effect" are post-fader, so that you can fade an instrument out of the mix and it won't continue echoing around in the reverb, delay, or whatever.

A pre-fader send gets its level from the preamp and/or EQ (if there is one). The level available to it remains constant. "Cue" sends, which are intended for creating the musicians' headphone mix, are pre-fader. This way, the musicians can hear a constant mix while the engineer is muting, soloing, panning, balancing, and so on. Sends marked "aux" or "auxiliary" are often pre-fader, as well.

The difference between pre- and post-fader sends has creative, as well as technical, implications. Imagine a song that stays in one key or mode, with a droning rhythm guitar part that strums throughout. It would be nice to send this guitar to a long, deep reverb so that the wet signal washes through the mix. Using a

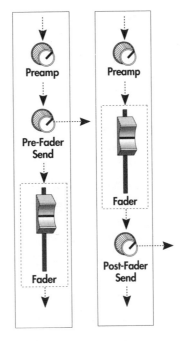

Fig. 3-6. Pre-fader and post-fader sends: The signal level available to a post-fader send is the level set by the fader, and changes when the fader moves. A pre-fader send gets its signal from the preamp and/or EQ, so the level available to it remains constant.

post-fader send, you could mix the track in a conventional manner, striking a good balance between wet and dry signals. But using a pre-fader send, you have the freedom to place the dry guitar at different levels for different parts of the song, or taking it out altogether, while the gentle wash of droning reverb continues undisturbed.

How Many? Like input channels, buses raise the question: How many is enough? Naturally, more is better. We can't all afford a humongous console, though, so following are a few guidelines.

As usual, the answer depends on the style of recording you do most often. If you record bands live to two tracks, or you mix MIDI sequences directly to stereo, you'll need more rotary effect buses and fewer switch-type tape sends. If you're recording live to multi-track, you'll need at least half as many sends as you have tracks of tape. If you tend to record one track at a time, tape sends shouldn't concern you (since you only need to route one bus to tape at a time), but rotary-style buses will become important when you mix. The more pre-mixing you do, the fewer sends you'll need, since you can use them over again with each submix. When mixing, a good bare minimum, generally, is two: one for reverb and one for delay.

Returns. Just about every send is paired with a *return* (or two, in the case of stereo returns). For instance, when you send a channel's signal to a processor via an effect send, the processor's stereo output is likely to be brought into the board via a stereo pair of effect returns. Likewise, if you send a channel's signal to a tape deck's input, you'll want to hear what comes back out of the tape deck via a tape return.

The fact is that returns are inputs, just like the mixer's channel inputs. They may look a little different, due to the board's layout, and they may be lacking EQ and sends of their own, but they're functionally equivalent to channel inputs and, in a pinch, can be used that way. On the other hand, you may want to return an effect via a channel input in order to take advantage of EQ, feedback (sending a bit of the bus output back into the bus), or some other channel feature.

Pan and Stereo Bus. The final stage of each mixer channel is a pan knob that distributes the channel's signal to the mixer's master stereo output bus. The pan knob is just like two rotary sends collapsed into one: As you turn it to either side, it raises one level and lowers the other. At the center position, it sends an equal level to both sides.

Likewise, the stereo bus consists of two buses like any others, except that they aren't paired with returns. This dual bus is intended to be routed to the studio's monitor amplifier, so that you can hear a combined mix of all the mixer's channels and returns. It never needs to return to the mixer.

Any bus, however, can function as a master output. Here's an idea: If you have a spare stereo amp and speakers in the closet, try using two effect sends in addition to the board's master stereo outputs to create quadrophonic mixdowns. (A 4-track machine is, of course, perfectly suited to recording quad mixes.) You may never go back to stereo.

Survey of Signal Processing

➤ A flood of information about signal processing has appeared in print in recent times. Surely electric guitarists, who employ stomp boxes of every shade and flavor to shape their tone, are already pretty well-informed on the subject.

Still, a lot has changed in the past several years, and many of the signal-processing applications used in recording require a more generalized approach than those commonly used with a guitar. At the same time, older forms of processing go out of fashion (anyone remember the ring modulator?). They're still valuable colors in the recording engineer's palette, though, and it can be helpful to consider them as you equip your studio.

In many situations (particularly at home, where high fidelity isn't a given) processing is the stuff that satisfying mixes are made of. For the time being, we'll simply cover the range of technical, practical, and creative possibilities for signal processing. Later, we'll look in depth at the types that are more or less indispensable.

Limiters and Compressors. A limiter puts a ceiling on how loud a signal can get, stopping it when it gets to a level, set by the user, called the threshold. This keeps signals that have unpredictable peaks—usually vocals, but often acoustic guitars and other instruments—from exceeding the headroom of your board, tape deck, or other devices, which would result in bad distortion.

A compressor is similar, except that it clamps down on the signal more gently when it exceeds the threshold, yielding a less controlled, but more natural, sound. How tightly it clamps down is determined by the compression ratio. Very high compression ratios are, for practical purposes, identical to limiting. Vocals, bass, guitar, and the full mix are the most commonly compressed signals, but just about everything gets clamped once in a while.

Delay-Based Effects (see Fig. 3-7). Delay creates a wide range of effects, including flanging, chorusing, repeat effects, and reverb. Flanging and chorusing are identical processes using different delay times. A delay unit gives you flanging effects if the delay time is set below, say, 20ms (ms is short for milliseconds, or thousandths of a second), and chorusing if the delay time is set between 20ms and 50ms. The delay time must be swept by a low-frequency oscillator, or LFO—usually built into the unit—to produce these effects.

With delay times in excess of

Fig. 3-7. Time-Based Effects: Flanging, chorusing, delay, and reverb are all created by delaying a signal by varying degrees. Delay times below 20ms create flanging effects (which can be made more intense by modulating the delay time by a low-frequency sine-wave oscillator). Between 20ms and 50ms, the effect is called chorusing, which is also subject to LFO modulation. In excess of 50ms, the delay is perceptible as a distinct repeat. When numerous delays are spaced very closely in time over a relatively long period, the result is reverb.

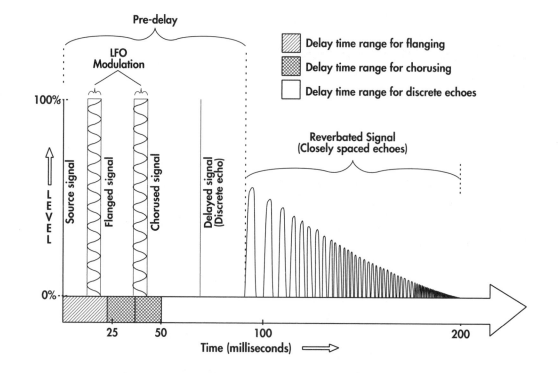

50ms, the delay ceases to mesh with the source signal and tends to sound like an echo. This is the conventional repeat effect, used to simulate doubling and to produce discrete echoes. Feeding the delay unit's output back into its input—there's usually an onboard circuit for this, although you can do it at the mixing board if you want—produces multiple repeating echoes.

Reverb (at least the digital variety) is nothing more than a huge number of closely spaced echoes. Spring and plate reverb units use different means to produce a similar effect. Often, there's a longer delay, called *predelay*, before the onset of reverberation, used to simulate larger spaces.

While the various delay-based effects are quite distinct in sound, they all tend to function as sonic "thickening," producing a fuller,

more animated sound. They can do wonders to fill out an otherwise sparse mix.

Phase Shifters. The phaser is really a poor man's flanger, but the effect is produced by different technological means and has its own distinctive flavor. In some cases it may even be preferable, especially since you hear a lot of flanging these days, and very little phasing.

Pitch Transposers (Harmonizers). A pitch transposer is a digital sampler that operates, more or less, in real time. "More or less" because the process inevitably introduces a slight delay. As it records, it can repeat individual sample points here and there, which lowers the pitch, or drop sample points out, which raises it.

Only a few musicians really put these devices to work, among them guitarists David Torn and Trevor Rabin and trumpeters Jon Hassell and Mark Isham, so the field is wide open for creative applications. This is particularly true with the advent of a new class of "intelligent" pitch transposers, capable of shifting by major or minor intervals in keeping with the key you're playing in. Many new-breed pitch transposers produce multiple pitches at once, deriving chords from a single-note input.

Octave Dividers. These devices, the poor man's pitch transposers produce a synthesized tone one or two octaves below the input signal's pitch. Some are built into fuzz boxes.

Equalizers, Filters, and Wah-Wahs. It's worth emphasizing that EQ can be used both to enhance the output from other effects, and as an effect in itself. Filters, which are like equalizers that cut sharply above a user-selected frequency, are standard equipment on most synthesizers. The filters on old-fashioned modular-style synths can be used to process external signals in unusual ways.

Guitarists are most likely to have encountered filters in the form of stomp boxes known as envelope followers, or envelope-controlled filters. These devices use the input's level to control the filter's cutoff point, often in an inverse relationship (as the input's level dies out, the filter sweeps upward, creating an effect usually associated with synthesizers).

An envelope follower's sound might be described as an automatic wah-wah effect. In fact, a wah-wah is actually a specialized kind of equalizer. It emphasizes only a narrow band of the frequency spectrum. When you work the pedal, you sweep that band up and down.

Enhancers, Exciters, and Imagers. These are the oddballs of the signal-processing world: All they do is make a signal sound "better." How they do it doesn't really matter; the result is usually brighter and perceptually (though sometimes not actually) louder. These babies can do wonders to perk up a dull instrument or mix.

Envelope Shapers. This category includes anything that allows you to drastically change the level of a signal over time, including volume pedals and noise gates. Guitarists tend to use volume controls to slow the attack of a picked note, but there are many other applications. During a mix, a pedal can be used to selectively fade an effect—say, distortion—in and out under the unprocessed sound, to add an unnatural articulation to a vocal, or for other creative effects.

Noise gates provide a different kind of control. In the usual application, the gate opens to let a signal through only while the signal is above a threshold level. When the input level drops below the threshold, the gate closes (at a rate determined by a release-time setting), so no signal gets through. When the threshold is set just above the noise level of a recorded track, the gate keeps the noise from being heard while the instrument isn't playing. This is great for getting rid of the grunge that often pours out of an amplifier when you overdrive it. (The

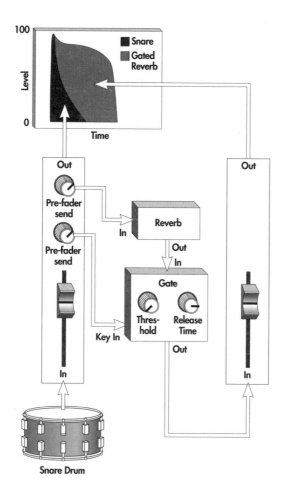

Fig. 3-8. The Famous Phil Collins Gated-Reverb Drum Sound: The snare's signal is routed to both the reverb and the gate's key input. The reverb output is fed into the gate's audio input. The gate's threshold should be set relatively low, and its release time relatively long.

grunge only disappears while the instrument isn't playing; when it plays, you have to depend on the sound itself to mask whatever noise is present.)

A *key input* enhances the creative potential of a gate. This kind of input—very different from the gate's audio input—pushes the gate open and closed in response to a signal *other than the one being gated.*

This is how the famous Phil Collins gated-reverb drum sound was produced (in the days before it was available as a program in a digital box): Reverb alone was sent to the audio input of a gate set with a medium-long release time, while the drum signal was fed to both the reverb and the key input (see Fig. 3-8). Thus, the reverb followed the contour of the drum itself, lasting just a little longer due to the release time setting. Mixing the straight snare with the output of the gate produces the familiar explosive effect. Potentially, any signal can key the gating of any other signal, opening a huge territory of creative possibilities. A hi-hat can key a gated keyboard pad. A rhythmic guitar might key sustained background vocals. A guitar solo could key a percolating synthesizer accompaniment. You get the picture.

Noise Reduction. Noise reduction can be useful as an effect. Dolby A and B lend themselves most readily to this, since they produce a bright, airy sort of distortion that can be musically appropriate. If one of your tape decks has Dolby or dbx noise reduction that can be switched on and off, try recording with it on and playing back with it off.

Vocoders. Usually, vocoders are used to create a robot-voice effect by imposing the harmonic content of speech on a synthesizer's output. Fortunately, this is just about the least interesting thing they can do.

A vocoder has two inputs—a *carrier*, which you hear at the output in altered form, and a *program*, which does the altering. The device derives the program's spectral characteristics and filters the carrier accordingly. Using a percussive program (such as a drum or a chunky rhythm guitar) and a sustained carrier (a synth string pad, a ringing guitar, background vocals, etc.) seems to work best, but almost any two signals will do the trick. A very underused set of effects.

Ring Modulators. Another way of combining two input signals: The inputs are processed in such a way that the output's spectral content consists of the sums and differences, mathematically speaking, of the frequency components in the program and carrier signals. Pretty abstract, huh? To put it simply, a ring modulator messes up the sound in a harsh but interesting way.

This effect is also underused, particularly by guitarists. A good reference is Jan Hammer's Fender Rhodes solo on "Red Baron" from Billy Cobham's *Spectrum* album.

Fuzztones. The familiar sound of overdrive distortion is a result of clipping, which occurs in just about any analog electronic circuit if you give it enough juice. Virtually any audio device can be overdriven to produce its own idiosyncratic distortion, which may or may not sound good to you. In most cases, it won't hurt to try. At the other end of the scale, there's a new generation of high-quality tube preamps that produce distortion effects previously available only with a megawatt amplifier, a stack of speakers, and a hardy microphone.

MIDI Control. MIDI isn't a type of effect. It stands for Musical Instrument Digital Interface: a standardized

digital code designed specifically for controlling musical devices, regardless of their manufacturer. The most basic kind of MIDI control is program-change capability; the ability to send, from a MIDI switching device, a command that reconfigures the processor for a new effect. Another basic application might be to control the mix of wet (processed) and dry (unprocessed) signals, or overall volume, via a MIDI foot pedal.

Some manufacturers allow the user to control various processor parameters in real time from a MIDI controller such as a keyboard, MIDI guitar, or sequencer. In a delay unit, for instance, these might include delay time, LFO modulation speed, filter cut-off, and so forth. The creative possibilities of this sort of control have yet to be fully explored.

Multiple Simultaneous Effects (Multi-Effects). Aside from MIDI and ever-increasing bang for the buck, the most interesting recent development in signal processors is the advent of devices capable of performing two or more processes simultaneously—reverb plus flanging, distortion plus chorusing, delay plus pitch transposition, and so on, from one box. Cost-effective, convenient, simple, and creatively stimulating. What more could you ask for?

Keep in mind, though, that such effects are digitally produced, and are subject to the limitations of digital technology. The more effects going at once, the more computations must be carried out by the unit's microprocessor, and the faster the microprocessor must be to put out a good-sounding signal. If it's not fast enough, you'll get your effects, but the sound may be compromised. As always, listen before you buy.

Food For Thought. That's it for the survey. Here are a couple of things to keep in mind as you explore the world of signal processing:

• Any processor can be used as an effect. Most processor types were invented to solve a specific technical problem—unwanted noise in the case of gates, for instance—but there's no rule that says you can't use them for their own sake.

• Don't hesitate to try an effect not usually associated with a given instrument—run a vocal through your fuzz box, flange a kick drum, pitch-shift the bass at the interval of a major second, delay the entire mix. Such unusual applications will make your music sound more unique and, as you accumulate experience, help you learn to apply effects more sensitively and intelligently.

• Consider that any time you process a signal, it exists in two forms: processed and unprocessed. Blending the two is a useful technique, both for creating subtlety and for making your stereo mixes more dynamic. Whenever possible, keep both processed and unprocessed versions of a signal available individually at the mixing board.

• Interesting results can follow from running a signal through several processors. The order in which you connect them has a big influence over the effect you end up with. Think the signal chain through first, so that you have some idea of what you're after. Then try all possible combinations to see what you can actually get.

• In a home situation, whether to process signals at the multi-track stage or during the mix is an important decision. Going to tape with processing gives you exact repeatability of sounds, and allows you to use a single unit differently on different instruments. On the other hand, it limits your flexibility later in the production. The choice depends on your setup, your style of working, and the demands of the music.

Recording Without Microphones: The Direct-Inject Technique

➤ In the dark days before the electric guitar, microphones were the only way to get sounds onto tape. The advent of instruments that generate electrical signals rather than acoustic sounds changed all of that. In this age of electric guitars and basses, synthesizers, samplers, and even electronic drum kits, microphones are no longer absolutely necessary. With electric and electronic instruments, there's no need to capture vibrations in the air and transduce them; the sound begins as an electronic signal, and it can go directly to tape without ever moving any air.

This is known as "going direct"—specifically, routing a signal source directly to a tape machine's input. An electric guitar's output can be recorded directly without any processing. This produces a clean, crisp sound, but it's not ideal because of the guitar's low output level and wide dynamic range. A preamp, EQ, and/or compressor will make the guitar's signal more manageable in this case. A more effective method is to tap the "preamp out" jack of an amplifier, which steps the guitar's output up to line level and may offer overdrive, equalization, and even digital effects such as reverb and delay. A multi-effects box can provide the necessary signal processing with greater flexibility. Alternatively, several processors can be linked sequentially.

For the sake of flexibility, not to mention capturing the nuances of their personal sound, all guitarists had better know a thing or two about microphones. But over the past several years, going direct has become more and more viable. These days, it can even be advantageous. This is particularly true if you (1) play electric or acoustic with a contact mike or similar transducer, (2) work alone, and (3) don't need to record vocals.

Going direct can save you a lot of trouble, since you can dispense with choosing the right type of mike, selecting a pickup pattern, positioning the mike properly, dealing with the acoustic characteristics of the room in which the mike is placed, avoiding phase cancellation when using two or more mikes simultaneously, and so on (see the section on mike placement). Generally, it results in a different quality of sound, opening up new creative possibilities, particularly in the recording of electric guitars.

When To Do It. Whether to use a mike or go direct is often an aesthetic decision. It depends on what equipment you have, what kind of sound you want, and what kinds of sounds you've gotten in the past using either method. They can sound very different—miking is generally warmer and less distinct, while direct is hard-edged, clean, and cold. Moreover, going direct can reduce background noise and often increases frequency bandwidth and transient response. Direct signals also seem to respond more readily to shaping via EQ and placement via reverbs and delays. Experiment until you have a clear idea of the differences.

Obviously, whenever the sound is perfect in the air, a good, well-situated mike will capture it best. Generally, under hi-fi, pro-quality circumstances, a mike yields richer and more subtle sounds than a direct line—if you have the room acoustics, equipment, and engineering talent to back it up. Many engineers prefer to record both direct and miked signals so that they can choose between them or mix the two.

Any time you don't have a mixer or a multi-track recorder and you need to record a bunch of players at once, the only choice is to put up a mike or two. With a mixer and/or a multi-track machine, if your intent is to capture a band's true live sound, you'll probably want to mike each instrument. If you play acoustic guitar and don't like the sound of a contact pickup, naturally a mike is for you—or if the other instruments in your group are primarily acoustic, or if you sing. Of course, if you already own a microphone, you might as well begin by using it. Using it a lot, that is, experimenting with various placements and sound sources to get

a feel for how it can be most useful to you.

Just about any other time, consider going direct:

• Whenever you have a spare track of tape, an input channel on your mixer, and the proper outboard equipment for shaping the sound of your guitar.

• Whenever your background noise situation makes miking impractical.

• Whenever your only option for monitoring is a speaker (that is, no headphones are available), and using a microphone would produce feedback.

• Whenever a decent mike simply isn't available.

• Whenever you want that squeaky-clean direct-inject sound. For distorted sounds, you'll need an amplifier with an overdrive control and a preamp-out jack, a Rockman-type device, a multi-effects box, or just a 20-year-old fuzz. For clean sounds, all you need is a compressor, perhaps an equalizer, and maybe a chorus or a flanger.

Effects. Reverb and delay make all the difference when recording direct. Without these kinds of processing, the sound has no "space" around it. After all, a signal coming out of your guitar, through a distortion or chorus device, and into a tape deck never really exists as a sound until well after it's been recorded. It's a signal, pure and simple, and it'll sound like one—cold and a bit lifeless. Giving it a bed of reverb and/or a quick delay helps give it the quality of having kicked around among the walls of a room.

You may want to add the reverb or delay as the signal is being recorded, but if you can, consider keeping the direct sound on its own track until mixdown time. This gives you the opportunity to shape the sound when it's in the proper musical context.

Thank You, Tom Scholz. The device that made direct recording practical in just about any musical and technological situation was the Scholz Rockman (and the deluge of imitations that followed). Through signal processing, the Rockman produces a sound similar to that of a miked amp/speaker combo along with compression and delay. Its output can be plugged directly into a tape deck to produce classic electric guitar sounds previously obtainable only with a microphone, a combo amp, and a few outboard effects. And everything it does is available at the flick of a few switches. Totally simple—no fuss, no muss.

The Rockman is relatively inflexible and sounds a bit brittle, and once you've checked out the other options, you may be disillusioned with it. Still, for sheer simplicity and trouble-free recording of monster guitar sounds, this little box is without peer.

Multi-Effects. More recently, companies such as Roland, Yamaha, and DOD/DigiTech have applied the technology they've developed for line-level digital effects toward guitar-oriented multi-effects boxes. These deliver just about everything a guitarist might want—delay, reverb, flanging, pitch-shifting, compression, distortion, enhancement, EQ—usually all at once. Such devices tend to be packed with programs (preset configurations of their internal parameters) designed specifically for guitarists, and offer a great deal more flexibility than the Rockman. If you go in for one of these babies, you're likely to find yourself catapulted into the high-tech world of digital signal processing and MIDI. The learning curve in this territory can be steep, but the rewards are an enhanced sonic palette and an incredible degree of control over your sound.

Digital multi-effects boxes are generally inferior, to some degree, to single-effect devices of comparable quality. There's a simple explanation for this. Digital sound results from computations carried out by a microprocessor. For each effect, the microprocessor grinds through a different set of equations, and it can only crunch so fast. In order to get it to reproduce the interaction of, say, 10 effects without any perceptible delay, the microprocessor must cut a few corners. When you cut corners, you degrade sound quality. (On the other hand, the signal path is much cleaner in a multi-effects box, since the signal passes through only one device, rather than several.)

The solution, of course, is to use dedicated effects rather than try to get everything you need out of one box. Cheap stomp boxes are plentiful—you probably own several already—and relatively inexpensive, especially if you buy second-hand. If you have the money, it's a better idea to invest in a bunch of studio-oriented line-level devices, and use a high-quality tube preamp for distortion and to boost the guitar's output level. (If you can avoid it, it's best not to use guitar- and line-level effects in the same signal path. The final output level will be very difficult to control.)

Using dedicated effects sacrifices the convenience of the one-button, one-box approach. However, it has the advantage of making various processors available individually during a mixdown, when they'll come in handy for drums, vocals, and other non-guitar sounds.

Caveat Engineer. The problem with all of these methods, if you choose to consider it a problem, is that they simply aren't the "real thing." A box of silicon chips simply doesn't sound like an overdriven Marshall stack. Digital algorithms approximate the complexity and color of tubes, speakers, and microphones, often with stunning accuracy, but there's always going to be a difference. However, the tradeoff in convenience often makes up for any sonic shortcomings. If you choose a box that has the effects you need and sounds good to you, it's hard to go wrong.

When shopping for a direct-inject guitar processor, bring a portable tape deck to the store and record various devices. That way you can compare them apart from the pressure and compromised listening environment of the showroom floor. Take your time. Listen carefully. The extra effort will pay off.

Follow the Bouncing Track

➤ Bouncing, also known as *ping-ponging*, can be a life-saver if you're working with a limited number of tracks. This nifty technique allows you to pack any number of overdubs onto a single tape track. This comes in handy, particularly at home, where the number of available tracks rarely exceeds four or eight—well short of the professional 24-track standard (which, as often as not these days, soars to 48 tracks and higher). With several bounces, your 4-track machine can record scores of instrumental parts.

But as useful as it is, this technique has its drawbacks: First, it degrades the sound. The real trick isn't bouncing itself, but knowing how far you can go before you're doing your production more harm than good, and how to get the best

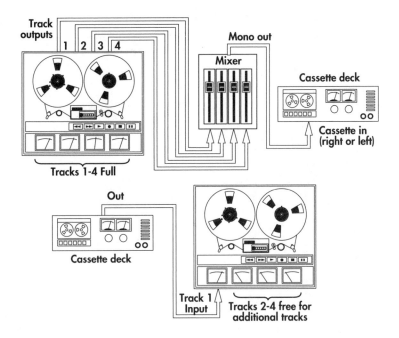

Fig. 3-9. Bouncing can be performed within a single multi-track deck, or between two decks. A pair of stereo cassette machines is fine for this purpose if you record a new track with each bounce.

results from each bounce so that you can keep the signal degradation under control. Second, once you bounce several tracks together, they're mixed for keeps. When several bounces contribute to the final production, it takes forethought, imagination, and experience to keep from mixing yourself into a black hole.

For the purposes of this discussion, I'll assume that you're working with an integrated 4-track cassette recorder/mixer. The principles apply to any tape format. If you have access to two tape decks, consider bouncing between them (see Fig. 3-9). A couple of cassette decks will work nicely for this. If you mix in a new performance with each bounce, two cassette machines make it possible to layer any number of overdubs.

How To Do It. The technique consists of mixing tracks that have

already been recorded, and recording the mix to a new track. Many 4-track cassette machines offer a switching configuration that feeds one side of the master stereo output bus to one track (or more). Thus, tracks 1, 2, and 3, once recorded, can be panned to one side and recorded—bounced—in mono onto track 4.

If your integrated recorder/mixer doesn't offer this option, it's easy to make the connection manually by routing a cable from one of the master outputs to the input of the track to which you want to bounce (see Fig. 3-10). Alternately, you can route an effect or aux bus to the track's input and mix via the sends. If you're using a multi-track deck with no mixing capabilities, you'll have to use a stand-alone mixer.

The Limits. You can repeat this process as many times as necessary, bouncing together tracks that are themselves made up of bounced

Fig. 3-10. If your integrated recorder/mixer doesn't have a switching configuration that allows bouncing from three tracks to one, it's easy to make the connection manually. Simply route a cable from one of the master outputs to the input of the track to which you want to bounce.

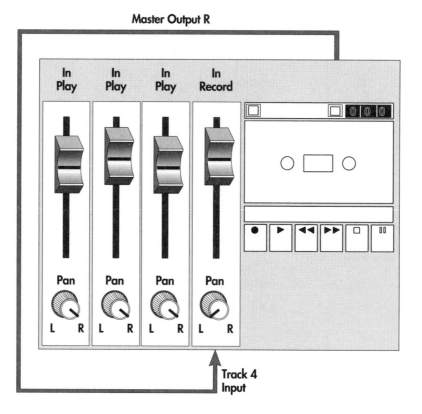

tracks *ad infinitum*. The first bounce, being a copy of previously recorded tracks, is known as a *second-generation* recording. If you record a few more tracks and then bounce them along with the earlier bounce, the original tracks will be in their third generation. The limiting factors are the tape hiss and distortion that build up with each successive generation.

This makes a lot of sense when you consider that in bouncing three tracks to one, you mix in three tracks' worth of tape hiss along with the music. As for distortion, if recording a signal inevitably distorts the signal a little, then re-recording a recording can only compound that distortion.

How much of this you can stand is a matter of personal preference. For some, any bouncing at all is too much. Most find the degradation intolerable after the second or third generation. Others layer tracks until the cows come home. In fact, excessive bouncing creates a sound of its own that you might find perfect for expressing a particular musical idea. Experiment to find out what effects are available and how much bouncing you can do and still maintain an acceptable level of fidelity.

Getting Around Them. In cassettes, the most obvious distortion occurs at either end of the frequency spectrum. High frequencies become weaker, or simply masked by hiss. The best way to handle this is by running the mixed tracks through an Exciter, or a similar device that generates high-frequency components, on their way to the new track.

At the other end, an emphasis tends to develop in the lower midrange, making the new track sound boomy. Use your ear to figure out where the emphasis is occurring, and pull back on that range with equalization during the bounce. If you take out roughly the amount added by the bounce, the new track will come out more or less flat.

Dealing with the added hiss is more problematic. It tends to be most audible in the high frequencies, so using EQ to roll off the highs can help. Unfortunately, this also rolls off the highs in the music. One way around this is to cut the highs with EQ and then regenerate them with an Exciter-type processor; if you do this properly, the Exciter should miss the noise and brighten only the music.

Another way to minimize tape hiss is to use EQ to over-brighten during recording (and/or during bouncing), and then cut the same range by the same amount upon playback. Thus, during playback the music ends up flat (more or less), while any added hiss is de-emphasized (see Fig. 3-11). The inherent noise and coloration (distortion) introduced by the equalizer itself, however, may create a questionable tradeoff.

One final comment: All processing more or less distorts the signal, inten-

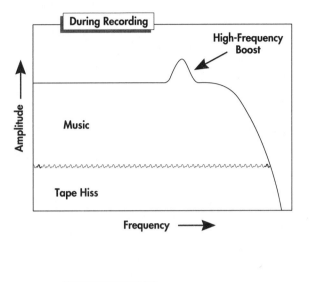

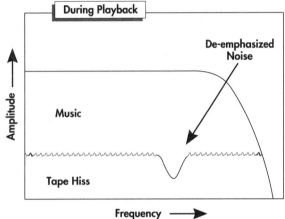

Fig. 3-11. It's possible to minimize tape hiss by using EQ to boost high frequencies excessively during recording (and/or during bouncing). During playback, cut the same range by the same amount. Thus, during playback the music ends up flat (more or less), while any added hiss is de-emphasized.

tionally or unintentionally. In strict terms, you'll always get the best result by recording clean, good-sounding tracks and leaving them alone. However, you'll never get a chorus of your own voice singing in 89-part harmony onto four tracks that way. In the world of home recording, it's one or the other.

Ten Parts On Four Tracks. Yup, you heard right: Ten instrumental parts, four tape tracks. And any given track is no more than *two* generations down. That seems a good compromise, no? Here's how it works (see

Fig. 3-12. Ten parts on four tracks, with no track more than two generations down: (1) Record tracks 1, 2, and 3. (2) Bounce 1, 2, and 3 to track 4. While bouncing, perform another part and mix it in That's four parts on track 4. (3) Record new parts on tracks 1 and 2. (4) Bounce 1 and 2 to track 3, adding another part in the process. That's three parts on track 3, for a total of seven parts. (5) Record a new part on track 2. (6) Bounce 2 to track 1, adding a part as you go We're up to nine parts. (7) Record a new part on track 2. That makes ten!

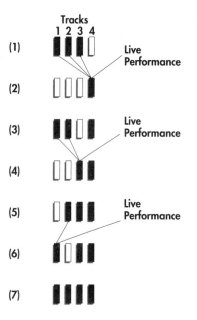

Fig. 3-12):

1. Record tracks 1, 2, and 3.

2. Bounce 1, 2, and 3 to track 4. While bouncing, perform another part and mix it in. That's four parts on track 4.

3. Record new parts on tracks 1 and 2.

4. Bounce 1 and 2 to track 3, adding another part in the process. That's three parts on track 3, for a total of seven parts.

5. Record a new part on track 2.

6. Bounce 2 to track 1, adding a part as you go. We're up to nine parts.

7. Record a new part on track 2. That makes ten.

But What About The Mix?

Technically, there's very little you can do to ensure that your bounces will add up to a good final mix. The best guides are intuition and experience. Keep in mind that you can remix a bounce as many times as you want before you decide that it's right. But after you record over the component tracks, you'll have to live with whatever you've done.

Add effects such as reverb, delay, chorusing, and so forth with each bounce, since you won't have an opportunity to apply them selectively later. Overcompensate for elements that will have to stand out in the final mix, such as kick and snare drums and lead vocals. Use equalization carefully to compensate for the distortion inherent in the process.

Plan track allocations in advance so that the most crucial parts—say, the lead vocal—end up on independent tracks. (In other words, in our seven-step example above, the lead vocal would have been the final track.) All bounced submixes will be in mono, so if you want certain elements to be panned opposite each other in the stereo field, make sure to bounce them to different tracks.

Doing the Old (Punch) In/Out

➤ Punching is one of the most powerful techniques in the recording engineer's bag of tricks. Next to overdubbing, it may be the most revolutionary development in analog recording technology—so revolutionary that it has become thoroughly taken for granted by engineers, musicians, and listeners alike. People were outraged when it was revealed, in late 1990, that Milli Vanilli didn't sing on their own records. Yet it doesn't seem to raise anyone's hackles that many of the most highly regarded performers rarely get through an entire take. Their "perfect" performances are actually patched together in a series of punches.

Most multi-track tape decks provide the ability to *punch in* to a previously recorded track, re-record a short segment, and then *punch out*, all without an audible interruption. The recorded performance to either side of the punch remains intact, making it possible to fix incidental flubs and other problems. The finished track is a composite of the best parts of what may have been dozens of takes, none of which was good enough to keep by itself. Lead vocals and instrumental solos seem to get this treatment most often. But the technique lends itself to just about any instrument or performance situation, and it's easy

to put to use in a home studio.

Basic Methods. Just about every recent multi-track machine, including the most modest 4-track cassette deck, makes punching fairly easy. With the relevant track record-enabled and playing back in sync (that is, monitoring from the record head), you simply hit record, or record and play, at the right moment. The machine switches from sync-play to record, capturing the new performance until you hit record (or play) again, at which time it switches back to sync-play.

Older machines may not make punching quite so convenient, but it's usually possible. For instance, the classic Teac A-3340 4-track reel-to-reel—still in use in a surprising number of home studios—doesn't allow you to record a track while it's playing in sync mode. Since hearing the track out of sync would confuse the musician, you have to start by switching the track-monitor function from "tape" to "source." Then you switch out of sync and into "normal" mode. *Then* you can punch in by hitting the record and play buttons. This isn't ideal—the player can't listen to the previous performance right up to the punch, because it takes a little time to switch from "tape" to "source," and from "sync" to "normal"—but it does work.

Likewise for punching out. If your machine doesn't let you punch out, simply stop the tape. This can be jarring, but it gets the job done.

Fine Points. The technique is simple, but requires a bit of finesse. After all, if you punch in too soon, or out too late, you'll record over the good parts of the take. A well-executed punch should be undetectable.

Picking good punch points is the key. Punching in and out during long silences gives you a lot of latitude, making it unlikely that you'll accidentally erase anything. If silences aren't available, listen for short breaks in musical phrases, moments when the vocalist pauses for breath or the guitarist changes position. If there are no breaks, the next-best thing is a change of chord or orchestration; say, the moment at which a new section of the song begins.

Don't even consider punching into a sustained chord (or note) unless you can afford to wreck the track. It almost never works. Usually, it leaves behind an ugly little glitch that sticks out like a pimple on the end of your nose. If there's no other choice, at least wait for the chord (or note) to change, and punch on that.

Keep in mind that the tape deck doesn't start and stop recording instantaneously. After you've hit the button, it takes a fraction of a second to engage. Thus, it's usually best to punch in slightly ahead of where you want to begin re-recording, and—even more important—to get back out with just a little time to

spare. Every tape deck has a different response time, so it may take a little experimentation to get the feel of yours.

Many professional decks have a "practice mode" that switches the monitor function when you punch in, but doesn't put the track into record. Unfortunately, in the semi-pro world, when you press record, you're in record. Getting it wrong can be disastrous, so don't be too shy to practice a few times by tapping your finger (or, better yet, flipping the track's monitor switch) at the appropriate moments.

Once the punch is complete, be sure to check it carefully. Listen not only for a good performance and a lack of glitches, but also for consistency of level, tone, and feel. Make sure your punch creates the illusion of a continuous performance.

Etiquette. Making great music is the goal, so it's important to be aware of the musician's experience while you're fixing the track, and to make him or her feel as comfortable as possible.

Before punching, let the performer(s) know where the punch will occur. It's usually best to have them start playing well before the punch-in point, so that they're already grooving by the time you hit the record button. Provide an adequate amount of playback time leading up to the punch, so they have a chance to lock into the feel. After each pass, let everyone know whether they should prepare to try again or simply listen back to the completed punch.

Under normal circumstances, the

THE RECORDING ENGINEER'S PALETTE   ↔   99

performer hears the previously recorded performance until the moment of the punch-in. At that time, his or her own instrument, sounding in real time, cuts in. Sometimes it's better to let the player hear him- or herself straight through (by leaving the monitor switch in "source"), while you execute the punch without hearing the results until afterward.

Alternatives. Punching isn't the only way to create a mistake-free composite track. In the lofty world of 24-, 32-, 48-, and 72-track recording, it's not uncommon to record a number of takes on separate tracks and cut them in and out during the mix. Obviously, you can do this with as few as four tracks, but it's not the most efficient method.

You don't need a mixer with channel mutes in order to give this a try. You can get in and out cleanly by switching the track between "source" and "tape" at the tape machine, and cross-fade among tracks using your mixing board's faders. You can even "automate" your composite by recording the result to yet another track.

Soldering Chops

➤ Anyone who's ever been in a rock and roll band—in fact, anyone who works with electric musical instruments at all—knows the famous corollary to Murphy's Law: The availability of a given cable is inversely proportional to your need for it. This is doubly true in the home recording studio. Cables are ridiculously expensive, so you tend to do without. Cable lengths never suit your needs, and their plug configurations never match your gear. And if you actually find a cable in your closet that looks like it'll do the job, chances are it's broken.

You can have the last laugh on old Murphy if you keep some soldering supplies in your studio, and develop some soldering chops. Broken cables? No problem—simply cut off the old plugs and attach some new ones. Need a cable that reaches from here to there? Cut a length from your roll of raw cable and solder on the plugs. Need a different plug type on one end? Exchange it with one from another cable.

Learning to solder requires a small investment in equipment and supplies, but it's enormously useful. It can get you out of tight scrapes during sessions, save you a few hundred bucks on big cable purchases, and

Fig. 3-13. Strip a portion of the outer sheath from the cable's other end. In most cases, 3/4" or so should do the trick.

lead you to more ambitious projects such as building a patch bay or repairing broken gear.

Step By Step. Making successful solder joints isn't difficult, but it does take care, patience, and practice. It's easy enough to try, though—all you really need is solder, an iron, some wire cutters, and a cable to take apart and put back together (no molded plastic ends, please). Consider including a little soldering workstation in your studio, where you keep the necessary tools and supplies and get your soldering done efficiently when the need arises. Keep a healthy supply of raw cable, plugs, and jacks in various formats. If you don't have room for a permanent soldering area, keep a small folding table on hand. Keep your tools in a plastic shoe box; the necessary parts can be stored in a small hardware caddy.

Here's a step-by-step approach that should get you off and running:

1. Gather the relevant supplies. These include the following:

• *Safety glasses.* Never, ever solder or cut wires without wearing safety glasses. Hot solder sometimes "spits," and small pieces of wire can fly when you snip. Wearing long pants and shoes is a good idea, too, to keep you from being burned by bits of stray

hot solder or flux.

• *Small wire cutter/stripper.*

• *Small needle-nose pliers.* These come in handy for holding onto hot plugs, for clamping down on recalcitrant wires, and for flattening bent surfaces. (Surgeon's hemostats are a good substitute, in some cases.)

• *Soldering iron.* Wattage makes a difference. An iron designed for delicate circuit-board work isn't likely to be powerful enough, while one with too much power will melt a wire's sheath. Between 30 and 45 watts is a good bet.

• *Soldering-iron stand.* This is simply a place to park the hot iron while you're paying attention to other things.

• *Sponge.* A small dampened sponge is a handy surface on which to clean the iron's tip as it becomes coated with ash and oxidation while you work.

• *Solder, tip tinner, flux paste.* Obviously, solder is necessary to the process. Always use rosin-core solder with a 60/40 lead-to-tin ratio. *Never use acid-core solder.* It's intended for heavy metal work (repairing downspouts and gutters, etc.), and will ruin your wires, plugs, and just about anything else. Tip tinner can rejuvenate an old iron when the tip has become tarnished, and flux paste helps with metal surfaces to which solder doesn't seem to want to stick. These items are optional.

• *Soldering jig* (optional). This is a set of robot arms with alligator clips for hands. They can hold a wire or piece of solder when your fingers are otherwise occupied.

• *Solder sucker* (optional). A small rubber squeeze-bulb, open at one end to create a vacuum. It can be used to suck up any molten solder that builds up over repeated attempts to make a connection.

• *Continuity tester* (optional). This is battery-operated box that lets you know when an electrical circuit between the two probes is completed. An ohm meter can serve the same purpose. Although I've marked this item as optional for soldering, it's something every serious studio owner should have on hand for chasing down faulty connections of all kinds.

• *Heat-shrinkable tubing and heat gun* (optional). This is for making tidy, short-proof connections. Made of a special type of plastic, heat-shrinkable tubing becomes smaller in diameter when heated. A heat gun is like a very powerful blow-drier. In fact, a good blow-drier may well do the job.

2. Cut a length of cable, and select two suitable plugs (one for each end, of course).

3. If the cable you're working with contains two or three strands of wire, the first task is to strip off a portion

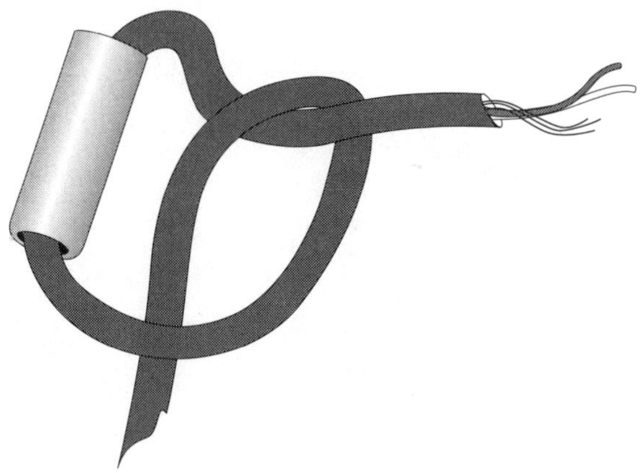

Fig. 3-14. Thread the cable through the plug's sleeve. It can be convenient to tie the cable in a loose knot, including the sleeve, so that it won't slide off the cable at the other end.

of the thick outer sheath (see Fig. 3-13). How much to take away depends on a combination of your personal technique and the size of the surfaces to which you're going to attach the wires. In most cases, 3/4" or so should do the trick.

4. Next, unscrew the plug's outer sleeve and thread the cable though it so that once you're finished soldering, you can screw the plug back together. It can be convenient to tie the cable in a loose knot, including the sleeve (see Fig. 3-14). This holds it in place so that it won't slide off the cable's other end.

5. The plug's internal structure is now exposed, and you should be able to trace the various lugs to specific points on the plug using your eye, or a continuity tester, if necessary (see Fig. 3-15). Tentatively line up the wires with the lugs. If the plug has a strain-relief clamp at its tail end, align the sheath with the clamp. Cut back the wires so that they're just long enough to make solid contact with their respective lugs.

6. Now it's time to strip the sheaths from each of the cable's indi-

Fig. 3-15. Trace the various lugs to specific points on the plug, using a continuity tester if necessary. If the plug has a strain-relief clamp at its tail end, align the sheath with the clamp.

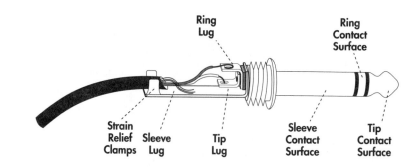

vidual wires. Don't go overboard! If two exposed wires touch, the plug will be useless, so you only want to expose enough bare wire to make contact with the relevant lug. About 1/8" is usually plenty.

7. To ensure a good solder joint, it's necessary first to *tin* each metal surface; that is, cover it with a thin layer of solder. To tin the individual wires, hold the soldering iron in one hand and the cable in the other; touch the iron to one of the wires, and the wire to the solder. (It can help to clamp the solder in a small vise or soldering jig, or you might want to try holding onto it with a spare finger.) Soon the solder will flow, covering the wire in a tidy layer. The procedure is exactly the same for the lugs: Touch the iron to the surface, and the surface to the solder.

Holding onto everything as you do this is a little like eating with chopsticks, and can take a little practice to coordinate. Everyone seems to do it a little differently.

Finally, tin the tip of the soldering iron by touching it to the solder. Wipe the tip on the dampened sponge.

8. Now you're ready to make the connection. Touch one of the tinned wire tips to a tinned lug, apply the soldering iron, and place the solder on the lug. (Once again, this takes some coordination. With practice, it will become more comfortable.) As soon as the solder flows, remove both iron and solder. The joint will solidify quickly. If you've done everything right, the connection will be permanent.

9. The joint should look tidy and, obviously, it should conduct electricity. Use a continuity tester or ohm meter to make sure it's doing so (see Fig. 3-16). It's easiest to set the tester to beep when its two probes are touching; otherwise, make sure its meter jumps.

To test a connection, hold one of the probes against one of the exposed wires at the far end of the cable. Hold the other against the part of the plug to which the wire in question is attached. The tester will respond if the connection is good.

10. If all is well, use pliers to crimp the strain-relief clamp snug against the cable's outer sheath.

11. On some plugs, the lugs are extremely close together. Cutting back the sheaths exposes too much wire, paving the way for the plug to short-circuit. In such cases it's appro-

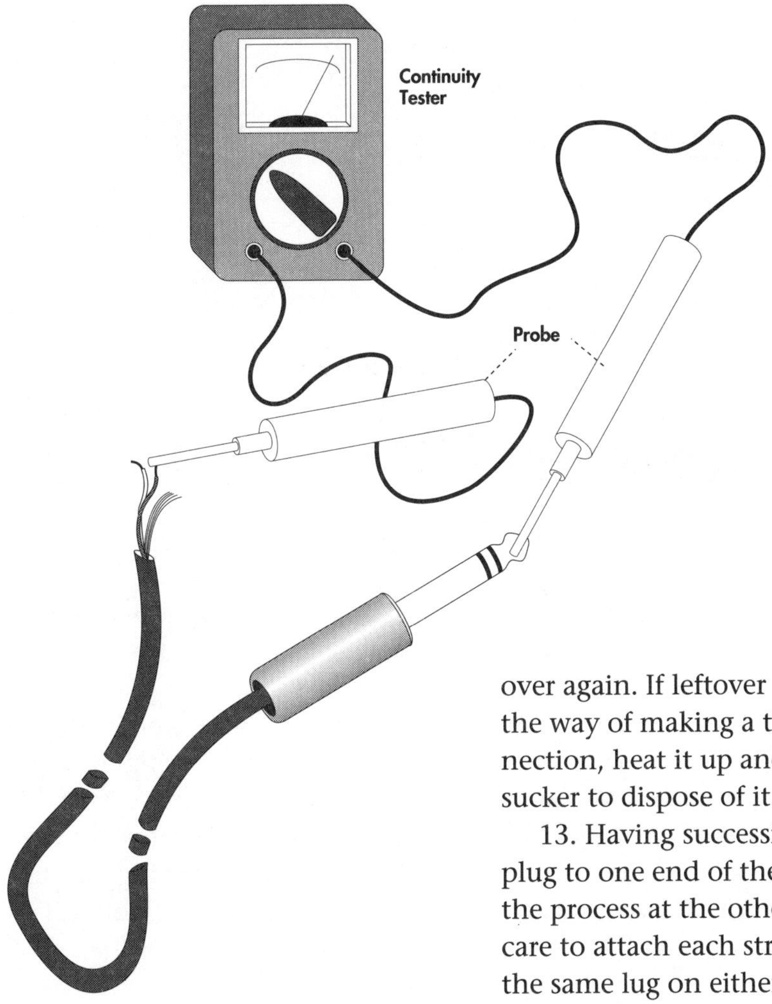

Continuity
Tester

Probe

Fig. 3-16. To test a connection using a continuity tester, hold one of the probes against one of the exposed wires at the far end of the cable. Hold the other probe against the part of the plug to which the wire in question is attached. The tester will respond if the connection is good.

priate to seal the connection within a bit of plastic, to make sure that two exposed wires can't possibly touch (see Fig. 3-17). Heat-shrink tubing is the ticket for this. Cut a number of small segments and slide one over each wire *before* you make the solder connection. Then slide it forward over the joint and shrink it using a heat gun. Use the heat gun sparingly to avoid melting the sheaths.

12. If things don't work out on your first try, don't worry. Remove the shrink tubing, reapply the iron, pull the connection apart, and start

over again. If leftover solder gets in the way of making a tidy new connection, heat it up and use a solder-sucker to dispose of it.

13. Having successfully attached a plug to one end of the cable, repeat the process at the other end. Take care to attach each strand of wire to the same lug on either end of the cable! When you're finished, you may want to verify the continuity by touching each probe of the continuity tester to the same part of both plugs.

Helpful Hints. Making good solder connections will be easier if you keep the following things in mind: Keep the portions of exposed wire as short as possible. Likewise, use as little solder as possible; too much solder can really muck up the job. Always tin all surfaces involved.

Apply heat as sparingly as possible. If you allow a wire to get too hot, you may melt away the sheath far-

Fig. 3-17. Make sure that two exposed wires can't possibly touch by sealing the connection using heat-shrink tubing. Cut a number of small segments and slide one over each wire before you make the solder connection. Then slide it forward over the joint and shrink it using a heat gun.

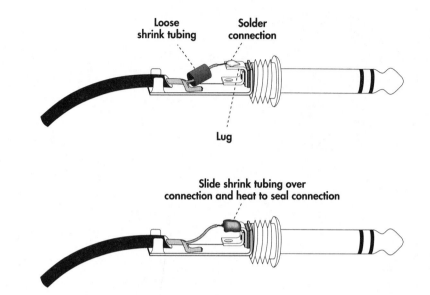

ther down the wire, possibly beneath the outer sheath, where you'll never be able to see the problem. This can cause mysterious short circuits.

Finally, when you're trying to melt the solder, heat one of the metal surfaces and touch the solder to it, rather than heating the solder directly with the iron. This causes the solder to fuse with the metal, rather than simply covering it in a separate layer.

Don't get upset if your first few tries aren't too successful. With a little practice your soldering technique will improve, and soon you may find yourself making cables just for the heck of it, instead of going out on Saturday nights. At that point, it's appropriate to start worrying.

Making the Connection:
A Survey of Cable, Plug, and Jack Types

➤ Sometimes it seems as though the studio is nothing more than a tangled mess of wires. But all of the cables begin at one point and terminate at the other, and they all carry a particular signal to its destination. That is to say, there's method to the madness. Here's a handy guide to some of the madness that comes up in dealing with various cable, plug, and jack types.

AC Cables. These come in 2- or 3-prong formats. The first and second prongs carry the "hot" and "neutral" aspects of alternating current. The third is connected to a wire that's designated as *ground*. Ground is an important and fairly abstract concept in electronics. Suffice it to say that, ideally, the ground in every device in your studio is connected to a metal post driven into the earth.

This isn't as impossible as it may sound. When an audio cable is plugged into a piece of gear, its ground contacts the device's own ground. The device's ground is connected to the ground pin on the AC plug. The AC plug connects to the AC receptacle, where the ground is connected behind the walls to a piece of metal in the ground (often the cold-water main).

Devices whose AC cables have only two prongs are said to have a *floating ground*. This can create problems, such as the dreaded hum of a ground loop, if there's a conflict with grounded devices. It can solve problems, as well; sometimes using a ground-lift adapter to bypass the third prong on a grounded AC cable can make a ground loop disappear. Discovering the source of a ground loop can be very difficult. If you have one that's particularly persistent, consider hiring a professional studio technician to chase it down for you.

And what about those little detachable DC power-supply transformers? These little nuisances have become ubiquitous in the home studio lately. From a manufacturer's point of view, they make great sense: They eliminate the need to get government approval for a device's power supply (which can be a time-consuming process), and to build alternate models to operate in countries that don't use the 60 Hz electrical standard favored in the U.S. Unfortunately, they're easily lost, easily tangled, and take up twice as much space on a multi-plug power strip as they should.

When you hook one of these to a

piece of gear for which it wasn't intended, be sure that you've matched two things: voltage and polarity. Voltage is easy enough. Simply make sure the voltage rating of the transformer matches the voltage requirements marked on the piece of equipment.

Matching polarity is more difficult. The connectors on these transformers aren't consistent, which means that they may deliver a positive charge where your equipment is expecting a negative charge, and vice-versa. This can cause irreparable damage, so be careful. Sometimes polarity is indicated by plus and minus signs on the transformer and the DC input of your equipment. If in doubt, check with the manufacturer.

Audio Cables. For the most part, audio cables contain two or three wires within an outer sheath. The sheath is plastic or rubber, and may be layered with a foil or braided-wire *shield* that helps to keep the cable from picking up radio-frequency interference (RFI, or simply RF) from the air like an antenna. The internal wires are also sheathed in plastic.

One of the wires is always dedicated to ground. If there are two wires, the other one carries the audio signal. If there are three, the cable is electrically *balanced*. Balancing is a clever electrical trick that eliminates RF and other extraneous noise picked up by the cable between one connection and the other.

The number of wires in a cable tells you nothing about the level or impedance the cable carries. You can make a good guess based on the plug configurations on either end, but it's still only a guess. When in doubt, check the owner's manual or call the manufacturer.

Plug and Jack Types. A variety of plugs is used in audio recording. Many are electrically equivalent, and are used for reasons of size, sturdiness, and similar practical factors. Here's a survey of the types you're likely to encounter. Since jack descriptions are more or less the same as plug descriptions, we'll only deal with plugs here.

Mono 1/4" phone. This is the most common audio plug format, the familiar connector on a guitar cable. It usually carries an unbalanced line-level signal, although in the case of guitars the level is much lower than line level.

Stereo 1/4" phone. You'll find this plug attached to a pair of stereo headphones. Although its design allows for a balanced mono signal, it almost always carries an unbalanced stereo signal. Headphones operate at a wide range of levels, depending on whether they're playing quietly or blasting.

Mono miniature phone ("mini"). These are rare, but crop up occasionally at the earphone output of small radios and cassette machines. The microphone inputs of such machines also use this format.

 *Stereo minia-ture phone.* The stereo head-phones that come with a Walkman or small radio usually use a stereo mini plug. Like the stereo 1/4", this plug can carry a balanced mono signal, but normally doesn't.

 *RCA.* You'll find RCA (or phono) plugs and jacks associated with home-stereo gear such as amplifiers, receivers, turntables, and cassette decks. Semi-pro recording gear employs them, as well, including the master outputs of mixers, 4-track cassette decks, and even some prefab patch bays. In just about every application except turntable outputs, these plugs carry a line-level signal, always unbalanced. They're not particularly sturdy or easy to pull in and out quickly.

 *XLR.* This is the standard format for low-impedance microphones. It's a heavy-duty balanced format, featuring three strong pins nestled within an indestructible metal shell. Balanced design and sturdy construction, along with the heavy-duty cable usually associated with it, make this format ideal for delicate low-level signals.

 *Ring-Tip-Sleeve.* Patch bays in professional studios often employ this heavy-duty format. The plugs are made of brass, and have three contact surfaces in order to route balanced signals at professional line level.

 *Balanced Bantam.* This is a miniature version of the ring-tip-sleeve format. Bantam plugs are also brass, and are also typically used for patch cords in the patch bays of pro studios.

 *Unbalanced Bantam.* A less common format, these plugs only have two contact surfaces. Home studios don't usually have many balanced signals running through them. Since many of the signals routed through a patch bay are unbalanced anyway, mono bantams are a good choice for a patch bay in a semi-pro environment.

MIDI. As MIDI (the musical instrument digital interface) becomes increasingly indispensable to all kinds of music-production work, MIDI cables proliferate. MIDI connectors belong to the category of DIN plugs, in which a circle encloses a number of delicate pins. Only three of MIDI's five pins are active. One is ground, and the other two carry a high-frequency digital signal. In general, MIDI cables shouldn't extend further than 20'; data errors accumulate in greater lengths.

Care and Feeding of the Home Studio

➤ If you have a gigantic pile of recording gear in your living room, you may wonder what it takes to keep it all performing up to spec. Fortunately, many studio devices consist of little more than a box full of silicon chips with virtually no moving parts to maintain and few contact surfaces to clean or replace. Provided you don't let them overheat, signal processors, computers, and other high-tech gadgets require virtually no attention. Microphones are relatively trouble-free—until they stop working altogether. Mixers require little more than an occasional squirt of contact cleaner around the faders and bus sends.

What will benefit from periodic care and feeding are your tape decks, both open-reel and cassette. If you own a tape machine, you ought to know at least how to keep its heads clean. Degaussing (demagnetizing) and aligning the heads are operations you may want to do without, or hire someone else to do, but it's good to be aware that they might be necessary from time to time.

Cleaning Heads. Whenever tape is rolling, it rubs against the deck's erase, record, and playback heads. Over time, the oxide particles that make up the tape's magnetic coating shed, and the heads become covered with them. This, of course, makes it difficult for the heads to do their job. Similarly, oxide particles rub off onto the machine parts that come into contact with the tape: the *tape guides, lifters, pinch roller* (the rubber thing that spins), *capstan* (the metal thing that spins against the pinch roller), and so forth. This interferes with the smooth and even motion of the tape across the heads. All of this explains why it's a good idea to clean your deck's heads and tape path before every session.

Audio supply stores sell head-cleaning kits, but you can do at least as well with Q-Tips and isopropyl alcohol. The alcohol should be as close as possible to 100% pure, so that it will evaporate quickly and won't leave any gunk behind on the head. (You can usually find 99% isopropyl alcohol at a pharmacy.)

After you've gathered the supplies, locate your tape deck's heads (see Fig. 3-18). They're small, flat surfaces—usually metal—that protrude from the middle of the tape path. Most open-reel machines have three, while most cassette decks have only two (one does double duty as both record and playback head).

Dampen a Q-Tip with alcohol and gently scrub the heads. Scrub vertically, across the direction in which

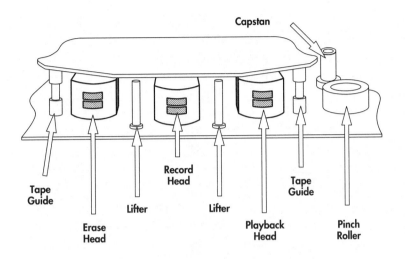

Capstan

Tape
Guide

Erase
Head

Lifter

Record
Head

Lifter

Playback
Head

Tape
Guide

Pinch
Roller

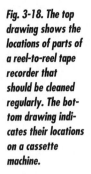

Fig. 3-18. The top
drawing shows the
locations of parts of
a reel-to-reel tape
recorder that
should be cleaned
regularly. The bot-
tom drawing indi-
cates their locations
on a cassette
machine.

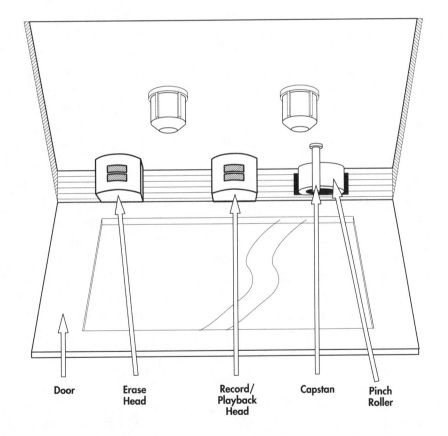

Door

Erase
Head

Record/
Playback
Head

Capstan

Pinch
Roller

the tape moves, to avoid damaging the head gap. Change Q-Tips when you can see the brown residue of oxide on the cotton swab.

When the heads are done, scrub all of the metal parts that come into contact with the tape. Rubber parts, which may be damaged by alcohol, are another matter. Try swabbing them, but quit if any rubber shows up on the Q-Tip. Cleaning the rubber pinch roller on a cassette deck is particularly tricky; I suggest you leave it alone unless the machine has been in use for several years. If you must clean it, remove the cotton head from a Q-Tip and use the stick to push the roller around carefully with one hand as you hold a moistened Q-Tip against it with the other.

There's a special method for cleaning an open-reel deck's capstan. Wet a Q-Tip and double it up with a dry one. The capstan spins whenever the right-hand tension bar is engaged, so push against the tension bar. As the capstan spins, touch the Q-Tips to its surface, keeping the dry one beneath the wet one. The dry cotton will absorb excess alcohol so that none of it seeps into the capstan motor.

Degaussing. Degaussing is just a fancy word for demagnetizing. Since a magnetic charge is constantly being passed through the heads while they're in use, a charge can build up within them. Likewise, a charge can build up in the metal parts of the tape path. The solution is to pass a degausser, which neutralizes nearby magnetic fields, along the tape path. This should be done from one end to the other in a single motion. Degaussers are inexpensive and easy to find at any electronics store that carries audio recording supplies.

There are three *very important* things to remember when handling a degausser:

1. Move it very slowly and smoothly whenever it's in the vicinity of a tape deck. Quick, jerky motions can induce, rather than eliminate, a magnetic charge.

2. Don't switch it on near the deck. Rather, turn it on about 4' away and move it into the vicinity of the deck with the slow, smooth motion mentioned above.

3. Keep the degausser away from VU meters. A magnetized needle can ruin a meter's accuracy. If the deck's VU meters are within 2" of the heads, it might be better not to degauss at all.

Because degaussing is such a fiddly process, and because, poorly done, it can make things worse than they were before, some professional recording engineers prefer not to fool with it at all. This seems a bit extreme to me, but it is what some people say. If you're feeling insecure about degaussing, perhaps the safest solution is to hire a professional to do the work for you.

Aligning Heads. Proper tape-head alignment ensures that the deck's frequency response is flat—that frequency components from the lowest to the highest get to tape at their original level, and that they play back from tape at the same level. This is achieved by adjusting small screws until the VU meters, during playback of a test tone, read zero. If you take your sound seriously, your tape decks should be aligned regularly. You might want to consider it every several months, depending on how much recording you do; in a professional environment, heads are aligned before each session.

Although I don't want to discourage anyone from doing his or her own alignments, it should be noted that aligning a tape deck can be an involved process, requiring a special set of test tones and separate procedures for the record and playback heads. Your deck's service manual (available from the manufacturer) will tell you how, if you're interested in doing it yourself. A multi-track cassette machine can be aligned by an authorized service center. If you have open-reel multi-track and stereo decks, you might want to ask a local recording outfit to recommend a good studio technician who can do the work for you.

Removing Tarnish and Dust.
Over time, tarnish builds up on just about every metal surface that's exposed to air. If an electrical contact's surfaces are covered with tarnish, the flow of electricity is compromised and may cease altogether. This is a common source of crackling and intermittent connections, particularly connections that otherwise appear to be sound.

You can deal with most of the problem by cleaning the audio plugs in your system regularly with garden-variety brass polish. This makes a huge difference if you have an extensive patch bay, since the patch cords are exposed to air much of the time. Give everything a good polishing every six months or so; you'll be surprised at how many of those inter-mittent connections clear right up.

Jacks pose less of a problem. There's friction against the entire contact surface of a jack whenever a plug is pushed in or pulled out, so jacks tend not to get so dirty. On the other hand, they're a good deal more difficult to clean. Pro-audio supply houses carry burnishing tools that scrape tarnish away. If you're dealing with jacks that have been sitting idle for years on end, you might have to start by fishing around with a Q-Tip dipped in brass polish. Be sure to clean off all of the polish when you're finished, though. If you leave it in the jack for a long period of time, it can corrode the metal.

Knobs, faders, and switches also get dirty. Every once in a while, you may notice that they crackle when you move them. This is nothing more than dust interfering with the electrical contacts. Much of the time, you can get rid of the crackling simply by working the pot up and down until you grind away the dirt. This works best after spraying the pot with contact cleaner, which can be bought at electronics supply stores such as Radio Shack. Be sure to get a brand that doesn't leave behind a residue, and apply liberally as necessary. This should keep your studio clean and crackle-free.

The Genteel Art of Microphone Placement

➤ A good recording begins with a good microphone. The placement of the mike in relation to the source, however, is just as important. This is particularly true in the often-compromised sonic environment of a home studio. The mike can't do it's job properly if it isn't placed properly, and the position can have a drastic effect on the sound it produces.

Standard mike placement techniques do exist, but there are no rules. Every engineer has his favorite placements, learned either by experience or from other engineers, but few would hesitate to modify them for each new track if something different were called for. The individual player's tone, the room, the number of other players in it, how they are situated, the musical context, the number of tracks available, and other such factors are the critical ingredients in mike-placement decisions, and obviously these vary a great deal from one situation to the next.

That said, let's take a look at some general concepts and principles that can serve as guidelines in coming up with good placements.

The Ear as a Microphone. This may sound obvious, but one of the best ways to position a microphone is to use your ears. Try thinking like a microphone. Point an ear at the source, close your eyes, and try different positions. Move the ear closer and farther from the source, as well as toward its various parts, paying special attention to any relevant orifices. Listen as accurately as possible. If you can hone your ear to the degree that you disregard all of the subjective factors that influence what you hear, you'll be hearing pretty much what a microphone would pick up. Really and truly, folks, this exercise can be very helpful. The only problem is getting the other musicians to stifle their laughter while you grope around the room with your head tilted and your eyes closed.

Proximity Effect. Ever notice how much meatier your voice sounds when you put your lips close to a vocal mike? Or how an acoustic guitar sounds too boomy when the mike is up close? The nearer most microphones are to the source, the more they emphasize the frequency spectrum's low end. This is known as the *proximity effect.*

You can take advantage of this to add boominess to a voice, to broaden the sound of an electric guitar, or to fatten a snare drum, but most of the time the proximity effect is less than desirable. It tends to make momen-

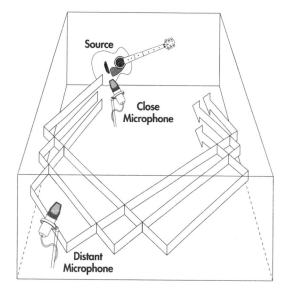

Fig. 4-1. Recording with two mikes: A close mike can be positioned to pick up only the sound directly generated by the sound source. A distant mike picks up mostly reflected sound bouncing off of walls, the floor, the ceiling, and other reflective surfaces in the room.

Source

Close Microphone

Distant Microphone

tary lows jump out in an unnatural way. Fortunately, it's easy to avoid. All you have to do is keep the source a short distance, say four inches or more, away from the mike.

Direct Versus Reflected Sound. The two major placement categories are close miking and distant miking, and the difference between them is largely the ratio of direct to reflected sound. With the mike close in, you get mostly sound emanating directly from the source. As you move the mike farther away, it picks up a greater percentage of the myriad reflections bouncing off the floor, walls, ceiling, and any other reflective objects in the room (see Fig. 4-1).

The limit of close miking is the size of the resonating body producing the sound. If the mike is extremely close to only a small portion of the source, it's not going to hear accurately those aspects of the sound being generated by the rest. A large bass drum is a good example. If the mike is too close, it won't pick up

the low frequencies that require some distance to get through their wave cycles, as well as resonances produced by the complex vibration of the drum head as a whole. Some engineers deal with this by placing the bass drum mike a few feet away from the drum and then enclosing the drum and mike in a tunnel made of blankets to maintain isolation.

The limit of distant miking is basically the noise floor of your recording system. If the mike is far enough away from the source, you'll have to boost its output a great deal in order to hear it; at the same time, you'll be boosting the noise inherent in the microphone/preamp/mixer/monitor system. Eventually, the added noise will outweigh the benefits of the reflected ambience you presumably wanted to record.

To the ear, the difference between direct and reflected sounds is obvious. Direct sound is "drier," more pointed and "present," and less complex. Reflected sound tends to be more ephemeral, less distinct, more subtle. If you record nothing but close-miked sounds, you'll probably want to add simulated reflected sound in the form of reverb and/or delay to substitute for the missing reflections. Otherwise, the recording may sound a bit lifeless.

During the '70s there was a stretch of time when acoustically dead (unreflective) studios and close-miked sounds were fashionable, as you can hear on records from that period. Since the '80s, the trend has been toward a much more live sound, in which mikes deliberately pointed toward reflective surfaces are mixed with closely placed mikes in order to preserve the sonically complex "room sound."

Feedback. Just about everyone who has been around microphones is familiar with the howl of feedback, and the damage it can do to speakers, amplifiers, and ears. Feedback occurs when the microphone's output is allowed to leak back into the mike, such as when a microphone is picking up the sound coming from speakers that are reproducing whatever the mike picks up.

The solution, of course, is to keep the speakers off whenever a mike is live (by listening via headphones), or by putting the mike in a separate room from the speakers. Feedback can be used to create wonderful musical effects, such as when a delay line is fed back into itself to create multiple repeats, but where mikes are concerned, it's strictly to be avoided.

Phase Cancellation. Sound waves bouncing off of various surfaces take different amounts of time to get to a microphone. Thus, the positive portion of a wave's cycle may arrive from one direction at the same time as the negative portion of the same waveform arrives from another direction (see Fig. 4-2). When this happens, the two versions of the wave are referred to as *out of phase*. When they combine, the out-of-phase waveforms add up to zero, cancelling each other out. The result? Well, if their amplitudes and shapes

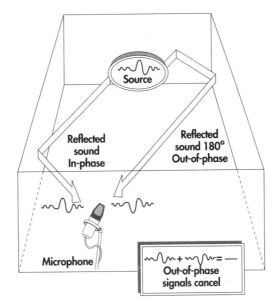

Fig. 4-2. Phase cancellation: When sounds from a given source bounce around in a room, they can be 180° out of phase when they meet at the microphone. When this happens, they cancel each other out.

are exactly the same, and they are exactly 90° out of phase, they cancel completely. The result, quite literally, is silence.

The unbelievers among you can confirm this for yourselves at any well-equipped pro studio by putting the console's built-in sine wave (intended for calibration purposes) on one channel, inverting its phase and sending it to the other channel at exactly the same level, and then alternately listening to it in stereo and in mono. When you switch to mono (combining the out-of-phase signals to one channel), the sound magically disappears. It reappears when you switch back to stereo.

In the real world of complex waveforms, multiple reflective surfaces, and idiosyncratic equipment, it's unlikely that anything will disappear, outright, from your speakers. You will, however, lose some frequency components of the sound to phase cancellation, while others are multiplied in loudness by the opposite of cancellation, *reinforcement* (which occurs when two identical, in-phase waves are combined). Call it what you want, but it can ruin your sound if you're not vigilant.

Some phase cancellation occurs whenever there are reflections in the room, but generally it takes place in such a small and random way that it actually spices up the sound rather than wrecking it. Phase cancellation becomes a potential problem when more than one mike is picking up the same source. It becomes even more problematic when more than two or more mikes picking up the same source are combined (that is, not strictly separated between the right and left channels).

Incidentally, similar phase problems crop up when you process the same signal through multiple reverbs and delays simultaneously, since these devices simulate the kind of room reflections picked up by microphones. If there's any chance your wonderful stereo recording will ever be listened to in mono, be sure to combine the channels and see if it still sounds acceptable. In many cases, it won't, and you'll have to reassign or eliminate the effects until it does.

Multiple Microphones. Phase cancellation is most troublesome in a stereo miking situation such as recording a solo acoustic guitar or piano, and whenever several mikes are used, as when miking a drum kit or a string section.

For stereo miking, the "3-to-1" formula is often recommended as a rule of thumb: In a stereo setup, the dis-

tance between the two mikes should be three times the distance of the mikes from the source. This is said to minimize phase cancellation, though I haven't tested it to any great degree. Stereo miking techniques that involve placing the microphones closer to each other may require more tweaking to set up. Always use your ears when positioning simultaneous mikes, and be on the alert for anything that sounds funky.

Using more than two mikes at once is usually a trial-and-error process. Most engineers, it appears, simply set them up and tinker around with the placement if any problems appear. I've read of systematic techniques for avoiding phase cancellation among a group of mikes, but most professional engineers don't bother with them.

Leakage. Multiple mikes may be trained on a single source, as in stereo miking, or they may be trained on various sources. This is the case with drums, where each mike may be listening to a different drum, and in a live band situation, where one mike is dedicated to the guitar amp, another to the bass amp, several to the drums, and so forth. In this case, another factor comes into play: *leakage,* sound from one source that finds its way into a microphone intended for another source.

There are two reasons to be concerned with leakage. First, there's the potential for phase cancellation, since two or more mikes are picking up the same source. Second, you lose control over individual sounds for purposes of mixing and applying after-the-fact effects. If the guitar is in the vocalist's mike, you're going to boost the guitar every time you turn up the vocal. Also, you're going to end up with delay and reverb on the guitar when you try to put those effects on the vocal.

There are several ways to reduce leakage. Through judicious placement of the instruments in the room, you can avoid pointing microphones in the direction of any but the sources you intend them for. Obviously, close miking thwarts leakage by minimizing reflected sound. Using mikes with cardioid and ultra-cardioid pickup patterns also helps, since those patterns tend to reject off-axis sounds.

Gobos, or baffles—panels padded with non-reflective materials such as soft fabrics—can be placed between instruments to block and absorb unwanted sounds. Similarly, blankets can be used to cover pianos, to wall off speakers, and so forth. Players equipped with headphone monitors can be placed in separate rooms or special isolation booths, although this tends to cut down on an ensemble's sense of togetherness.

Finally, a mike's signal can be routed through a noise gate. The gate closes when the input level drops below a set threshold level, shutting out the leakage (since it's likely that it won't be as loud as the intended source). When the intended source plays, the level jumps and the gate opens, letting the signal reach the tape deck. Using a gate eliminates leakage only when the source isn't active. Obviously, when the gate is open, everything comes through, including any leakage.

Miking Speakers. Here's a tip for miking combo amps and speakers. Rather than pointing the mike directly at the center of the speaker, point it slightly inward from the cone's edge, about 5" or 6" away. This keeps the mike from being hit with the full impact of the high sound pressure levels generated by a loud amp (which can be damaging), while allowing it to listen to the speaker up close.

Experiment! Now that you have some principles to go by, experiment with various mike positions. Try recording the same music with the mike(s) in various places, just to get a feel for the range of effects. Go wild! Record an acoustic fingerpicking passage with the mike 2" from your right hand, over the soundhole, pointing at your left hand, 3' away, 20' away, pointed at a distant corner of the room, 3" from a wall, down the hall—whatever you can imagine. Then do the same thing with another kind of source, such as a flute or a violin. If there aren't any other players around, use a radio or some other automatic sound source. When a player does step into the room, you'll be ready to capture his or her performance in all its excitement and nuance.

All Things Being Equalized

➤ All of the studio's tools are designed to help you control and manipulate the sounds you want to record and play back. None, however, deals with sound on as basic a level as the equalizer. You can think of the equalizer (EQ, to studio adepts) as a set of tone controls much like the bass and treble knobs on a common stereo amplifier. The difference lies in how accurately you can choose which areas of the sound you want to boost and/or cut.

In order to understand what an equalizer can and can't do, you may find it helpful to review the section on the physics of sound. Let's recap the relevant points: You hear a sound when the air molecules surrounding your ear vibrate. The speed at which vibrations take place is known as *frequency*. Frequency is the determining factor in the musical perception of *pitch*. Basically, low frequencies (slow vibrations) produce low pitches, and high frequencies (fast vibrations) produce high pitches.

In the real world, of course, it's not quite that cut-and-dried. Any pitched sound can be analyzed as a composite of a basic frequency, called the *fundamental*, and any number of higher frequencies, known variously as *overtones*, *partials*, or *harmonics*. The distinction is somewhat abstract, but you can hear it quite clearly. The

fundamental frequency is the pitch you recognize—the six pitches to which you tune the strings of your guitar, for example. The overtones create the sound's characteristic *timbre*, or tone color—the factors that let you tell the difference between, say, a clean guitar sound and one processed by a fuzz box.

Dividing the Frequency Spectrum. The range of all possible frequencies is called the *frequency spectrum*. The portion of the spectrum that humans can hear is known as the *audio spectrum*. In case you're wondering, the audio spectrum extends from 20 Hz to 20kHz (*kilo-Hertz*, or thousands of cycles per second). Any continuous portion of the frequency spectrum is called a *band*. It may be very wide—say, the entire audio spectrum. Or, it may be narrow, for example between 80 Hz and 600 Hz, the average range of the human voice's fundamental frequency. A band may even be as narrow as a precise fundamental frequency without any overtones, such as 440.00 Hz (the *A* above Middle *C*).

In any case, a band's narrowness or wideness, measured in Hertz, is called its *bandwidth*. Some equalizers give you control over the bandwidth of one or more bands. The general frequency of each band is determined by setting a *center frequency* that, appropriately, lies at the center of the band. Once the center frequency and bandwidth are set (assuming those parameters are variable), the band can be *boosted* (increased) or *cut* (decreased) in level. Fig. 4-3 shows the relationships of bandwidth, frequency, and boosting and cutting.

Manipulating the Spectrum. Now we're ready to bring EQ into the picture—not the real thing, but an imaginary equalizer. This equalizer has an unusually high degree of flexibility and precision.

Suppose you play the *A* above Middle *C* (440 Hz) using a bright sound with enough distortion to produce long sustain. Imagine that the equalizer allows you to set one of its center frequencies to 440 Hz, and that the bandwidth around that center frequency is ridiculously narrow—less than 1 Hz. Now boost the loudness of the center frequency by, say, 3dB (3 *decibels*, which may not sound like much, but which in many situations can be quite a lot).

What have we done to the sound? All we've done is alter the strength of the overtones relative to that of the fundamental. Since the fundamental is now 3dB louder, the overtones are effectively 3dB less loud, making our once-bright sound somewhat duller. If we wanted to, we could cut, rather

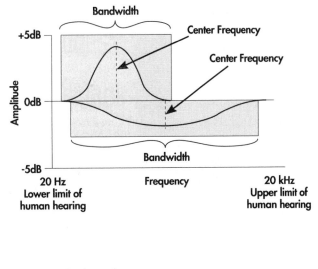

Fig. 4-3. An equalizer boosts or cuts the loudness of one or more bands, or divisions, of the frequency spectrum. The location of each band is determined by its center frequency and bandwidth. In some equalizers, the center frequencies and bandwidths are adjustable, while in others they are predetermined.

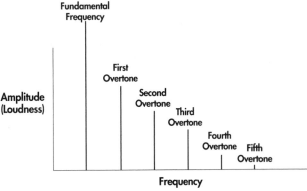

Fig. 4-4. Typical frequency components of a pitched sound, and their relative strengths. The fundamental is the loudest. The strength of the overtones is usually inversely proportional to their frequency.

than boost, the fundamental by 3dB. This would make the sound brighter, and also somewhat heavier, since the lower overtones would be emphasized along with the higher ones. Fig. 4-4 shows the relative strengths of overtones of a given fundamental frequency.

Change the center frequency on the imaginary equalizer to 8,440 Hz, that is, 8kHz above the fundamental. In this region of the frequency spectrum, you affect one or more of the higher overtones. Boost the band 3dB and the sound is brighter, since the upper overtones become louder relative to the fundamental.

Now, let's widen the bandwidth around the center frequency to 16kHz. Our boost of 3dB now affects the sound over a range of 8kHz in either direction. It boosts all of the overtones between the fundamental and 8,440 Hz (without affecting the fundamental itself), and also boosts the overtones from 8,440 Hz to 16,440 Hz, which approaches the upper limit of human hearing. We've effectively boosted everything except the fundamental, making the sound brighter and heavier—a more complicated way of achieving the same thing we did earlier when we isolated the fundamental and cut it by 3dB.

A More Complicated Scenario. Now imagine equalizing an entire mix rather than a single tone. This situation is much more complicated. By boosting or cutting a given band, we affect the relative loudness of the overtones related to several fundamentals simultaneously—not to mention that we affect *unpitched* sounds such as drums (and also any noise in the system).

It's likely that several pitches will be sounding simultaneously to form chords, creating an overlap among the overtones belonging to one fundamental and those belonging to another. In addition, since the fundamentals created by some instruments are presumably moving around to form melodies, your equalizer's center frequency and bandwidth—which are fixed, unless you twist the knobs in time with the music—will have a different impact on the sound with each new note played.

As you can see, equalization gives

you very precise control over sound, but even the fanciest equalizer has limitations built into the physics of sound itself. That's not a problem; it's simply the nature of the tool.

Types of Equalizers. There are two basic EQ designs: *graphic* and *parametric*. Graphic is simpler to understand. A graphic EQ divides the audio spectrum into a number of pre-set bands of equal width, and allows you to individually boost or cut each band. Naturally, the more bands and the greater the amount of boost and cut, the more precisely you can control the effect. Since the boost/cut amounts are usually determined by the positions of vertical sliders arranged side-by-side on the unit's front panel, a graphic EQ gives you a visual representation of how it alters the input; hence, the name "graphic." Outboard, stand-alone EQ units are usually of graphic design.

A parametric equalizer breaks the frequency spectrum into only a few bands, but gives you control over three *parameters* that define each band: center frequency, bandwidth, and boost/cut amount. While graphic EQs offer a wide but preset selection of center frequencies, parametrics allow you to zero in on precisely the frequency you want, such as the sizzle of a snare drum's snares. The width of each band on a graphic equalizer can't be changed, either, but with a parametric you can narrow the effect to emphasize just the brightest portion of the snares, or widen it to emphasize a broader, heavier part of the snare drum's spectrum. The boost/cut amount control

on a parametric is the same as the boost/cut control provided by graphic equalizers. The equalizers provided with each input channel of a mixing board are usually parametric.

A variation on the parametric concept is the *quasi-parametric* equalizer. A quasi-parametric may give you control over center frequencies but not bandwidths, or it may give you parametric control over the low-range and midrange bands while providing only boost and cut for the highs.

Which is better, graphic or parametric? Neither. Generally speaking, it doesn't even depend on the application. It's simply a matter of taste. Producer/recording artist Todd Rundgren had the board in his home studio modified to include graphics on each channel because he finds their operation more intuitive. I prefer the greater control afforded by a good parametric. Quasi-parametric designs often yield the best performance per dollar.

If you're in the market for an outboard equalizer, bear in mind that, as with any audio component, each individual model has its own sound. You may prefer a parametric design, but a comparably priced graphic model may have an overall sound that better suits your ear, or vice-versa.

EQ Techniques. It's nice to be able to show off in the studio by telling your producer that what the guitar sound *really* needs is about 3dB at 9.7kHz, but not everyone has that kind of ear. For EQ neophytes, here's a foolproof method for operating an equalizer.

Assuming there's an offending bandwidth somewhere in the sound, the idea is first to locate it, and then to deal with it properly:

1. To find it, start at a point obviously below it and boost successively higher bands. If you're using a graphic, this involves turning each boost/cut slider up and down in turn until the area of the sound you're interested in jumps out at you. On a parametric, simply crank up the boost knob and then sweep the range of center frequencies.

2. Once you've found the proper band, decide whether you need to affect a narrow bandwidth or a wider area. With a parametric, you can simply play with the bandwidth knob. With a graphic, you'll want to try turning up and down the bands on either side of the center frequency you've selected. Once you're satisfied, either boost or cut as needed.

Cut or Boost? One thing to remember as you're twisting the EQ knobs is that *a cut is as good as a boost*—even better, in fact, if it can achieve the effect you're looking for. Say you want to emphasize the upper mids. Rather than boosting the upper mids, try cutting the lower mids. Want to enhance the bass? Cut the treble. This is because any time you boost, even in a very narrow bandwidth, you raise the overall level of the signal. (It's easy to verify this by patching in a VU meter after the equalizer. You'll be surprised at how much level a little EQ adds.) If you're not careful, you may boost the overall level beyond the distortion tolerances of your gear without realizing it. It would be a drag to finally notice the distortion while you're playing your finished masterwork for the president of Warner Bros.

Also, any time you boost a signal, you boost some noise as well, both noise in the signal and noise in the EQ unit. So always consider cutting before you decide to boost.

Applications. Basically, equalization is applied in only two ways: to enhance a single instrument (or sound) in a mix, or to affect several instruments at once, often the entire mix. The reasons for equalizing an isolated instrument aren't obscure. The sound may need a little tweaking to make it fit in better with the rest of the mix, or it may simply be lacking in one area or another. You might even want to EQ an instrument as an effect, to make it sound uncharacteristically tinny or boomy, or to make it become progressively darker or brighter.

Why EQ an entire mix? There are a number of reasons, ranging from noise reduction to making tape copies sound better. It's less common to EQ a selected group of instruments within a mix, but you might want to do this if, say, you've overdubbed a single singer several times to create background vocals. In this case, the vocals will sound more monolithic if each vocal track is EQed in the same way.

Before we turn our attention away from the lowly equalizer, here's a list of specific applications. Some may be obvious, while others might suggest interesting avenues of experimentation.

• Equalizing in context: Rather than EQing instruments individually to make each one sound as full and rich as possible on its own, equalize them in the context of a mix. For instance, put the drums up before equalizing the bass and rhythm guitar. This way you're tailoring each instrument to fit into its own place, rather than forcing it to fight with other sounds occupying an overlapping aural "space."

• Improved cassette copies: Compare one of your masters with a cassette copy. Cassettes often have a little "bump" in the bass response—that is, a bit too much low end. Also, copies usually lack some punch in the highs, and are noisier. EQ the copy to sound as close as possible to the master. Now, whenever copying, route the original signal through the same EQ on its way to the cassette machine. This will compensate for the distortion.

• Noise reduction: When recording tracks, lay them down with an exaggerated boost in the highest possible range, preferably somewhere between 8kHz and 12kHz. Upon playback, cut the same band by the same amount. This will bring the recorded material back to its proper timbre while cutting in the general range of tape hiss. The result, of course, is less hiss. This is basically how Dolby noise reduction works.

• Simulated stereo: Stereoize a monaural signal by splitting it into two equalizers (see Fig. 4-5). Cut some frequencies and boost others

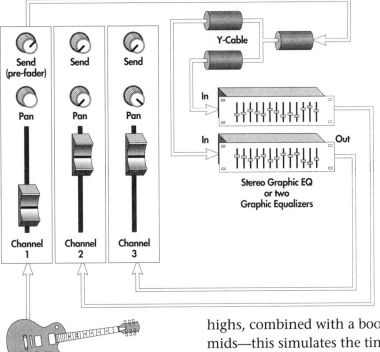

Fig. 4-5. A simu-
lated comb filter
for stereoizing a
mono source: The
guitar's signal is
not directly heard,
but is sent via a
pre-fader effect
send to two equal-
izers with opposite
boost and cut pat-
terns. The equalizer
outputs are panned
to opposite sides.

with one of the units; with the other, boost by the same amount those frequencies you just cut, and cut those you boosted. This is easiest with two graphic equalizers; simply boost and cut alternate bands on one, and reverse the boost/cut pattern on the other. Pan the outputs of the two units hard-right and -left. The signal will retain its sonic character, but will sound bigger and livelier.

• Dynamic EQ: Try changing EQ settings while a mix is in progress. You might try making the guitar progressively brighter throughout a solo, or mangling the vocal to emphasize particular words or phrases. Cutting the EQ in and out can also be effective. This technique is a favorite among dub (reggae) producers.

• EQ as distortion: The most commonly heard application in this area is extreme cutting of the lows and highs, combined with a boost in the mids—this simulates the tinny sound of a transistor radio. You might extend the technique by creating a similarly extreme emphasis in the low or high end. The transistor-radio effect can be heard at the beginning of "Wish You Were Here" by Pink Floyd and in the middle of "This Flight Tonight" by Joni Mitchell.

• Equalized effect sends: Reverb can be made much lighter-sounding and more subtle by routing the send through an equalizer and cutting the low end. In fact, if you still use a spring reverb because you can't afford a digital unit, this could make a big difference in the quality of your studio's sound; a judiciously EQed send can take most of the "sproing" out of a spring reverb. Unusual effects can be obtained by EQing the send to a delay line. In fact, any effect send can be equalized with interesting results. And don't forget to try EQing the return, as well.

Spinning the Web of Reverb

➤ Whenever a sound occurs, waves of motion in the surrounding air spread out from the sound's source in all directions. If you're up in the mountains and yell into a canyon, the waves travel to the far wall, bounce off of it, and return to you some time later sounding quite like the original yell—the familiar echo effect.

In an enclosed space, the interactions between sound waves and the surrounding environment are more complex. In a rectangular room, for example, a similar echo bounces off of the far wall, but it returns to the near wall and bounces again, and continues to bounce back and forth until its energy is dissipated. Meanwhile, the sound waves spread out at various angles from the near and far walls, bouncing off of the walls to either side, the ceiling, and the floor (see Fig. 4-6). Some frequencies are absorbed by soft surfaces such as curtains and furniture, while others bounce all the more energetically from concrete and wooden surfaces. As the sound bounces around the room, a complex web of densely packed echoes builds up and dies out, creating a phenomenon known as *reverberation*.

In a small room, this happens relatively quickly—so quickly that it usually escapes notice (unless the walls are made of some highly reflective material, such as smooth concrete). In a larger space, it can be quite noticeable, and quite distinctive.

Artificial reverberation, known as *reverb*, is more or less crucial to multitrack recording. In an overdubbing situation, the instruments in the ensemble perform separately, and never actually occupy the same room at the same time. In fact, some engineers and producers prefer to eliminate *all* influences of physical space when recording individual tracks. This is known as recording "dry," and allows the engineer to add an impression of space to taste as he mixes.

In any case, at any point in the production process, reverb can be added to a combination of tracks in order to group them, from the listener's perspective, in a single physical space. On the other hand, contrasting types of reverb can be applied to set various instruments apart. The simplest way to think about reverb is as the back-to-front complement to your mixer's panning knobs, allowing you to place instruments closer or farther away, rather than to the right or left.

Reverb Technology. Methods of creating reverb range from miking sounds as they bounce around an actual reverberant chamber to send-

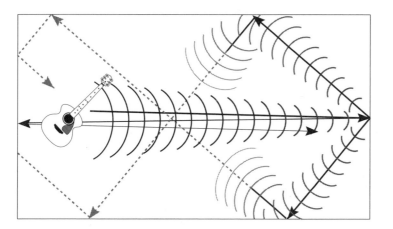

Fig. 4-6. Reverberations in an enclosed space: In a rectangular room, sound first bounces off of the far wall. It returns to the near wall and bounces again, and continues to bounce back and forth until its energy is dissipated. Meanwhile, the sound waves spread out at various angles from the near and far walls, bouncing off of the walls to either side, the ceiling, and the floor.

ing them through a metal spring and amplifying its vibrations. At this point, though, *digital* reverb has the field pretty much sewn up. It's inexpensive, hassle-free, and can sound far better than its predecessors.

Digital reverb works by processing digitized sound through a mathematical *algorithm* (formula) designed to simulate the effect of a specific acoustic environment. An algorithm often includes several variables, called *parameters*, that provide a degree of control over the effect. With a well-designed algorithm and high-quality digital signal-processing hardware, it's theoretically possible simulate the effect of any space from the dingiest public rest room to the grandest cathedral.

Keep in mind, though, that while digital reverbs may offer programs called "Carnegie Hall" and "Tiled Bathroom," the contents of those programs bear only the most abstract relationship to Carnegie Hall and a real tiled bathroom. There's no acoustical photograph of Carnegie Hall in the box. The program is intended to simulate the object named, and may do it accurately, fancifully, or just

plain poorly.

On the other hand, a box may include algorithms (as opposed to programs) named "Concert Hall" and "Small Room." Here, the distinction may be quite meaningful. Such algorithms configure the microprocessor's resources to carry out mathematical operations that have proven relevant to simulating the characteristics of hall- or room-type spaces. Like programs, algorithms bear no direct relationship to their names, but their names are probably based on a more rigorous analysis.

The least expensive models offer only preset effects, without any variable parameters. Since the hardware required for most digital effects is identical, such units often boost their appeal by providing delay, chorus, flanging, pitch shifting, and other effects in addition to reverb. These units are usually great bargains, but they're by no means equivalent to their more costly competition. The difference between low- and high-priced reverb is often a matter of the quality of the A-to-D and D-to-A convertors, processor speed, and on-board RAM (random-access memory),

Fig. 4-7. Early reflections give way to more closely spaced reflections that soon become so dense, they can't be individually distinguished.

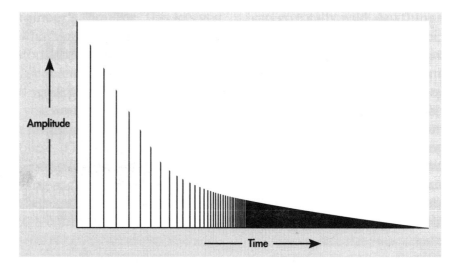

so more expensive models tend to deliver higher-quality audio and a great deal more flexibility. One of the simplest ways to dramatically improve your studio's sound is to upgrade the reverb, so it pays not to skimp.

Reverb Parameters. In the natural world, reverb doesn't follow a sound immediately. Rather, it builds up over a short time. In a large space, it takes a moment for sound to bounce off the far wall and back to the source, which must happen before more complex interactions can take place. In studio lingo, this time period is known as *pre-delay*. It's a simple characteristic to add to any reverb device that lacks it, digital or otherwise—simply route the send through a delay on its way to the reverb. The longer the delay (within reason), the larger the space will appear to be.

The pre-delay is but the first of several initial echoes coming from various walls. These are known as *early reflections*. If the sound origi-nates at the front of a large hall, the second and third reflections tend to come from sound bouncing off of the walls to the right and left, and are simulated by delay lines panned to the left and right.

Since some high-frequency energy tends to be absorbed with each bounce of the sound waves (depending on the texture and composition of the walls), the various reflections often become increasingly dull. Digital reverbs simulate this by passing the outputs from various delay routines through a *lowpass filter* (sometimes called a *high-cut filter*). Likewise, the reflections become less loud as they diffuse throughout the room. This may be determined by a *feedback*, or *regeneration*, parameter.

Early reflections give way to more closely spaced reflections that soon become so dense, they can't be individually distinguished (see Fig. 4-7). Various room characteristics influence the reverberation during this phase. A room's size and the reflec-tiveness of its surfaces determine how

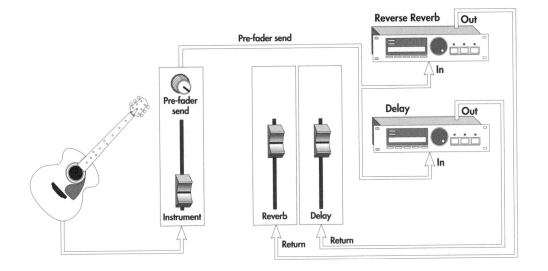

Pre-fader send

Reverse Reverb | **Out**

In

Delay | **Out**

In

Pre-fader send

Instrument

Reverb | Delay

Return | Return

Fig. 4-8. The "reverse reverb" effect included in many digital reverbs can be made more useful in conjunction with a delay line. In some musical contexts, it's possible to delay the track you're interested in reverse-reverbing so that it syncs with the reversed effect properly. Be sure to delay the track only in the monitor, and not in the reverb send.

dense the reverb becomes, how quickly it reaches maximum density, how long it lasts, and how long it takes various frequency ranges to die out. These may be reflected in a digital algorithm as *reverb time, room size, low-, mid-,* and *high-frequency reverb time, attack, definition,* and so forth.

The most basic reverb parameter is the one that controls the wet/dry mix. The ratio of *wet* (processed) to *dry* (original) signals determines how near or far away the sound appears to be, and how a particular simulated space compares to others in the mix. If you're using a mixer's effect send/return bus to add reverb to your mixes, this parameter should be set for 100% wet signal; the mixer's reverb return knob will control the wet/dry mix. If you route your mixer's master outputs through the reverb unit on its way to the mixdown deck, it's necessary to adjust the wet/dry mix on the unit itself.

Gated Reverb. Most digital reverbs include an algorithm for *gated reverb*. Back in the pre-digital

days, this effect was created by routing a reverberator's output into a noise gate and *keying* (triggering) the gate via the reverb send (see p. 86). With a snare drum, this arrangement lets a powerful explosion of reverb through the gate with each drum strike, which cuts off abruptly as the gate closes. The effect is so common nowadays that its inclusion in the digital palette is *de rigueur*.

Reverse Reverb. Another common feature is *reverse reverb*. This simply causes the usual mathematical calculations to be carried out in reverse order, creating a "reverberation" that swells dramatically from diffused tail to hard initial reflection. The swell necessarily occurs after the sound itself, rather than leading up to it, which makes this effect less useful than it might seem. In some musical contexts, it's possible to delay the track you're interested in reverse-reverbing (delay it in the monitor, that is, not at the effect send) so that it syncs with the reversed effect properly (see Fig. 4-8).

To obtain a true reverse reverb, or *preverb*, it's necessary to turn a tape with recorded tracks over so that they play backwards. Send the tracks to a reverberator, and record normal reverb on another track. When you play the tape in the proper direction, the reverb track will foreshadow every sound on the original tracks in a most intriguing manner.

Using Reverb Effectively. There are really no rules for putting reverb to good use. It helps to visualize the spaces in which you want the music to take place. Try to be aware of how much reverb is necessary to achieve a natural sound, and use more only when you really want to create an effect.

Experiment with using different reverbs (and delays) on different instruments to create a sense that the music is happening in several contrasting spaces. Do a few mixes with no reverb at all, just to remind yourself that dryness has a character of its own. When you get tired of that, go overboard and throw "too much" reverb on selected elements in the mix. With a little practice, you'll find that reverb can be the crucial factor that differentiates a lifeless recording from one that truly breathes with a life of its own.

Using Delay Effectively

➤ One of the mixdown engineer's most powerful allies is the lowly delay line—a device that repeats a bit of musical material after a given time interval. Delay effects can be subtle or drastic; it's a good bet that you're hearing them in every modern recording of popular music. Very short delays usually show up as flanging and chorusing. Longer delays sound like a stutter, and still longer ones like an echoing repeat. (The term "echo," however, often refers to reverb rather than delay.)

Anatomy of a Delay Line. Delay lines come in both analog and digital flavors. The most common form of analog delay is *tape delay*, which takes advantage of the distance between conventional record and playback heads to produce the effect. As tape rolls, a signal is encoded at the moment it passes over the record head. Some period of time later, as the tape passes over the playback head, the signal is reproduced. The slower the tape speed, and the farther apart the record and playback

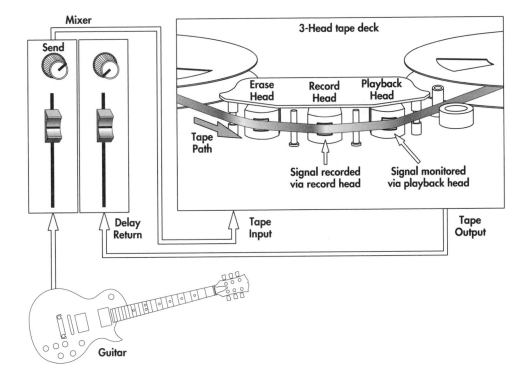

Fig. 4-9. Tape delay takes advantage of the physical space between a tape deck's record and playback heads.

heads, the longer the delay time. Old-fashioned delays such as the famous Echoplex and Roland Space Echo operate according to this principle, and any three-head tape deck can be used the same way (see Fig. 4-9). Stomp-box analog delays use non-digital electronic components to "remember" an input signal for a short period of time, and then pass it along to the output.

A digital delay line (sometimes called a *DDL*) converts analog input signals into digital data and stores them in random-access memory (RAM). This is the same technology used in digital samplers and computer-based digital recorders. Unlike the stomp-box type of analog delay, DDLs can hold the digitized sound in memory indefinitely before passing it on (although many manufacturers don't design their products to do so).

The length of the delay is dependent on the amount of RAM, the sampling rate, and the triggering mechanism. DDLs tend to offer the widest range of delay times, as well as other functions based on digital technology, such as one-shot sampling.

Delay Variables. The most basic delay line parameter is, of course, *delay time*, which is usually adjustable via a knob or increment/decrement switches on the device's front panel. The device usually records the incoming signal for the length of the delay time, after which it immediately plays back the recording. Both recording and playback are continuous, however, so every sound that goes in comes back out, sooner or later.

Most delay devices allow you to modulate the delay time with a low-frequency sine wave generated by an

Fig. 4-10. Internal regeneration provides a mix of the delay's output and the input signal.

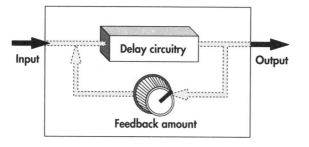

on-board low-frequency oscillator, or *LFO*. This is like a robot hand that twists the delay-time knob back and forth. The speed with which the "hand" sweeps is the *modulation rate*, and how far back and forth it moves is the *modulation depth*. Continuous alteration of the delay time has the effect of raising and lowering the pitch of the delayed output. The pitch stabilizes only when the delay time comes to rest. A high setting for the modulation amount, or depth, makes for jarring, wobbly pitch variations. Low settings create more subtle effects.

Feedback, or *regeneration*, is another standard delay feature. This simply mixes some of the device's output back into its input (see Fig. 4-10). The delayed signal is passed to the output as usual, but also feeds back into the delay line to be delayed again, and again, and again—the standard multiple repeat effect. It can be convenient to route this feedback loop externally, rather than using the device's internal signal routing, so that you can control feedback from the mixing console (see Fig. 4-11).

Many delay devices offer *lowpass filtering,* as well. This is basically a tone control that removes some of the output's high-frequency content, making it sound duller than the original signal. Filtering makes the echoes die away more naturally, much as they would if you were to shout into the Grand Canyon. It also helps to keep the echoes from interfering with other elements in the mix.

As with any effect, an important consideration is the relative amount of wet (delayed) and dry (undelayed) signals—controlled by either the *output mix* or *balance* knob, or by the delay return at the board. A quick slap often works best when the delayed and undelayed signals are of equal strength, for instance, while a long delay may be most effective when it's barely audible in the mix.

Delay Effects. Delay applications divide quite naturally into effects involving very quick, medium, and very long delay times (see Fig. 3-7 on p. 84). Very quick delays, when mixed with the dry signal, tend to vary the tone color of the original sound, rather than sounding like a repetition of it. This is the realm of flanging and chorusing. As the delay time increases, the wet signal begins to differentiate itself from the dry signal to be heard as a discrete echo. Right at this boundary, the combined wet/dry mix results in a particularly fat sound. Just beyond it, the delayed signal creates a distinct "slap-back" echo, suggesting a small, enclosed space. When the delay is long enough to be heard as a distinct time interval, it tends to give the feeling of a large, unenclosed space.

Flanging and Chorusing.

When a signal is delayed between 1ms and 20ms, with a slowly modulating delay time, and mixed half-and-half with the dry signal, it takes on the characteristic *whoosh* of *flanging*. In addition to the tone color it imparts, flanging can be useful for giving a background texture, such as an arpeggiating electric guitar, added definition. Also, panning flanged and straight versions of a signal to the right and left creates a spacious stereo spread.

Slightly longer delay times—say, up to 30ms—with a little more modulation tend to make a signal sound double-tracked. This is known as *chorusing* (as in a chorus of voices) because it tends to sound like more than one instrument playing the same part. Panned to the center, the delayed and undelayed signals combine to create a strong, thick texture. Panned to either side, they can produce a full, spacious mix.

Flanging and chorusing effects range from mellow to vibrantly animated, depending on the modulation rate and amount. Adding some regeneration tends to make the sound edgy. Even more regeneration produces a gritty, metallic effect.

Without modulation and with the mix 100% wet, delay times in the flanging/chorusing range can be used to alter the rhythmic placement of an instrument—that is, to make it lay a bit behind the beat. Applied to a hi-

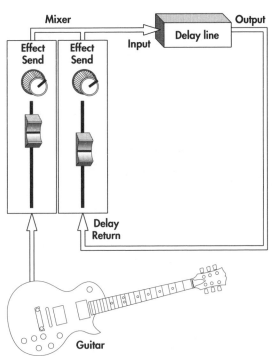

Fig. 4-11. Regeneration can be controlled externally from the mixing console, rather than from the delay's internal feedback circuit.

hat or a shaker, this can be useful for loosening up a stiff drum machine program, particularly with a tiny bit of delay-time modulation.

Slap-Back. Between 30ms and 60ms, delay begins to assert itself as a sonic element apart from the input—but not quite. As the delayed sound becomes apparent to the ear, panning becomes less a psychoacoustic effect than a matter of the overall instrumental arrangement's right/left balance.

Carefully adjusted, with a nearly equal wet/dry mix and no modulation or regeneration, this kind of delay blends with the input, extending it in time. Panned to the center, this is great for adding weight to a solo line or a lead vocal. Panned apart, this gives the part lots of definition, making it stand out in the mix. This kind of delay is commonly applied to the damped single-note rhythm guitar part on R&B records; it's good for fattening a snare drum, as well.

A slightly longer delay with no modulation or regeneration produces the classic '50s-style slap-back, in which the delay is just barely recognizable as a separate element in the mix. This is a common sound for guitar solos, chunky rhythm guitars, and vocals. A small amount of delay-time modulation can make sustained parts, such as pads, appear to soar as their pitch bends ever so slightly.

On rock and roll records from the '50s, you occasionally hear a slap applied to the mix as a whole. This can make for an energetic and unusual, if slightly chaotic, mix. With careful application of regeneration, a slap-length delay makes a crude but useful reverb—but only in a pinch.

Long Delays. This category includes delay times equal to or in excess of the length of a sixteenth-note. Delays in intervals of even divisions, or multiples, of the music's basic pulse—that is, sixteenth-notes, eighth-notes, quarter-notes, half-notes, and so forth—can be very useful. With no regeneration, they can add rhythmic interest to most percussion parts, single-note lines, or punchy rhythm parts. With regeneration, particularly in longer note values, they can wring a full-sounding mix from a sparse arrangement. Carefully mixed, they can also create a sense of depth that is more felt than heard.

This is one reason to avoid preset digital effects boxes that offer a zillion programs, but don't allow you to set the delay time independently. Unless one of the manufacturer-determined delay times happens to match the tempo of your music, this kind of application is out of the question.

When applied to drum and percussion parts, rhythmic delays can be used to produce interesting grooves and feels. Setting a delay to a dotted rhythm, with or without regeneration, can be particularly effective in this regard. Experimentation is really the only way to scope out the possibilities for a given rhythm track.

In most cases, you'll probably want the delay to be as rhythmically accurate as possible. If you don't, or if you can't get it absolutely right, it usually sounds better if the delay is a little too long, rather than a little too short. Long delays, especially in excess of a quarter-note (one beat), can be useful when they're out of time, as well. This tends to create a sense of space and excitement, and is a common effect for lead guitars and vocals. Patching the delay output to a fader, rather than an effect return, makes it easy to fade the echoes up only at the ends of phrases, lending drama to a mix without drowning it in a wash of delays.

In most delay applications, the wet/dry balance tends to favor the dry signal, with the echo(es) dying away more softly. Keep in mind, however, that unusual effects can be produced by making the echo louder than the original signal. The break in Led Zeppelin's "Whole Lotta Love,"

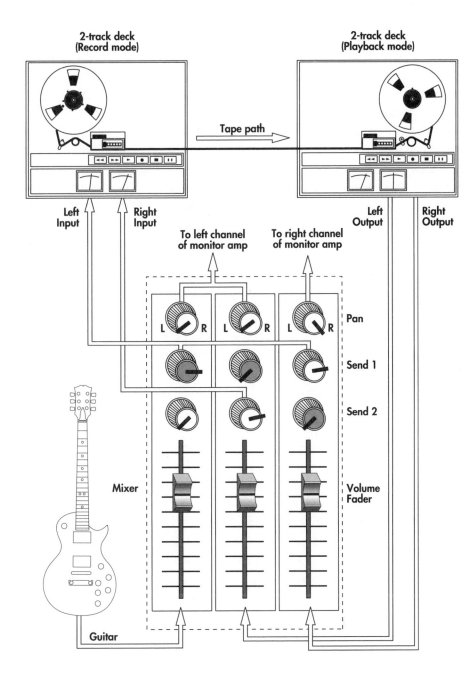

2-track deck
(Record mode)

2-track deck
(Playback mode)

Tape path

Left Input

Right Input

To left channel of monitor amp

To right channel of monitor amp

Left Output

Right Output

Pan

Send 1

Send 2

Mixer

Volume Fader

Guitar

Fig. 4-12. Creative signal routing for mondo delay fun: the Frippertronic tape delay system using two stereo tape decks, patched so that the repetitions bounce across the stereo field.

in which the echo of Robert Plant's voice is louder than the voice itself, is a good example.

Frippertronics. The ultimate long-delay application is the celebrated "Frippertronic" technique, refined by the transcendent fretmaster Robert Fripp. This simply involves

using a very long delay—several seconds, at least—with as much regeneration as possible, short of runaway feedback, as a tool for creating canonic compositions. Fripp's system involves placing two tape machines several feet apart, threading them with the same piece of tape, and recording onto one machine while playing back with the other, at the same time mixing the second machine's output back into first's input—a mondo tape-delay system. By routing the signal properly between two stereo decks, you can make the echoes bounce between the right and left channels for a very spacious sonic environment (see Fig. 4-12).

High-quality tape machines produce the best-sounding Frippertronics, but you can create much the same situation using a long digital delay such as Digitech's 7.6-second Time Machine. Either way, it's highly recommended as a way to create unique textures, or simply to have some great fun playing your instrument.

Compression: The Audio Shoehorn

➤ In today's microprocessor-mad world, one item that tends to get overlooked is the compressor. Compression comes in handy in many situations, but it's particularly crucial when you're recording guitars or vocals. If you're trying to do serious, pro-quality recording at home, you can't afford to do without a compressor. (If you're not ready to buy, consider renting from a local studio or audio-rental house for crucial sessions.)

Just as an equalizer is useful in shaping the frequency content (timbre) of a sound, a compressor offers some control over its amplitude, or loudness (see Fig. 4-13). You might look at it as a smart volume knob or fader—one with a robot hand that pushes it up and down in response to

the strength of the signal itself. When things begin to get too loud, the robot hand pulls the volume down; as the sound dies out, it pushes it back up.

The operative concept is *gain reduction*. You might consider this to be the opposite of amplification. Regardless of its absolute level, a signal going into a compressor can be considered to be at 0dB—that is, no boost or cut. As it gets louder, the compressor pulls it back proportionately, reducing gain. As it gets softer again, the compressor returns the amount of gain to normal.

Since musicians spend years learning to control the dynamic characteristics of their performance—that is, the moment-to-moment variations in the loudness they generate—compression may not look so appetizing from a musical point of view. In recording, however, it facilitates a necessary process: shoehorning the potentially infinite dynamic range of acoustic sounds into the distinctly limited dynamic range of magnetic tape. Moreover, it gives you creative control in shaping sounds to suit the needs of the production.

Controls. Compressors have few controls and are fairly simple to operate. Most of the time the effect is subtle, though, so it may take a bit of practice to learn to use it effectively.

The *threshold* control sets the level above which gain reduction takes place. If you wanted to keep a few incidental peaks in a rhythm guitar under control, you would set a relatively high threshold, so that only the peaks would be compressed. On the other hand, if you wanted to make a blazing solo leap out of the mix, you might set the threshold relatively low so that every note is affected.

The *ratio* control determines the amount of gain reduction you get when the input signal exceeds the threshold. For example, if the ratio is 2:1, the unit will provide 1dB of reduction for every 2dB of input level beyond the threshold. (That is, if the input exceeds the threshold by 20 dB, the compressor's output will only go up 10dB.) This holds back the peaks fairly gently. A ratio of 6:1 clamps down pretty hard on levels beyond the threshold. At about 10:1,

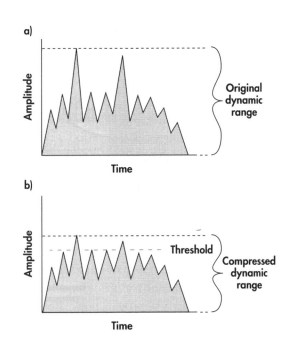

Fig. 4-13. A signal enters a compressor with its original dynamic characteristics, or changes in amplitude (a). It leaves with a narrower dynamic range (b).

the effect is no longer considered compression, but rather *limiting*. That is, the signal is given a ceiling above which it simply cannot stray.

Attack time determines how quickly the compression kicks in, allowing you to compress fairly heavily and yet retain the distinctive attack of each individual note. Likewise, *release time* determines how readily the compressor lets up. With heavy compression, too quick a release can make the sound seem to swell paradoxically as it dies away. Too slow a release can cause the material following a big peak to get caught in the compression effect, even though it isn't above the threshold. These kinds of effects, in which the fluctuations in gain are noticeably unnatural, are known as *pumping,* or *breathing.*

Most audio devices include an *output gain* control, but it's particularly helpful with a compressor. At low-threshold/high-ratio settings, the compression effect may drastically reduce a signal's average level. It's more or less necessary to have a preamp built in to bring everything back up to a practical level.

A compressor's meters may show you the input level, the output level, or the amount of gain reduction (preferably switchable between all three). In the latter case, the compressor's meter, whether VU-style or a line of LEDs, begins at "full up" and moves downward with each peak of the input signal. This gives you a pretty good idea of what the compressor is doing if you're having trouble hearing the effect plainly.

Applications. On the large time scale of seconds and minutes, compression smooths out the dynamic range of a performance, so that its loudest moments stand out less from its overall volume. A skilled vocalist, for instance, often produces a swell of volume as he or she sustains a note. Although this may be musically appropriate, it can create problems for a recording engineer. If you mix the vocal so that it sounds right when the swell is at its peak, for example, it's likely that some of the words will drop below audibility from time to time. On the other hand, if you mix the vocal so that every word is intelligible, the sustained notes may overwhelm the track. Using compression, you can narrow the dynamic range so that the vocal maintains a good position in the mix at all times.

On the other hand, untrained vocalists often are all over the map when it comes to the consistency of their volume level. One word comes out a mumble, while another is a meter-pinning shriek. If the musical goal is to create a vague, disorganized, raw sound, this is fine. But if you want to be able to hear what the vocalist is doing at all times, compression is in order.

On the small time-scale of fractions of a second, compression can have a subtle but important effect on an instrument's presence. You can use it to change the relationship between, say, the sound of picking and that of the guitar's ringing strings, emphasizing one or the other. This is particularly useful with bass sounds, where compression can de-emphasize the attack and bring out the body of each note. Compressing drum sounds softens the impact, but makes each strike last a hair longer, so the drums occupy more space.

The danger, of course, is that you'll flatten a performer's artistry into an overly homogenized mass of sound—not an uncommon result in this age of techno-overkill. But with musical sensitivity and a little practice, it's not difficult to use compression to retain the best characteristics of a performance while making it blend nicely with the other instruments.

It's not uncommon to compress an entire mix. This technique takes advantage of the pumping phenomenon in order to crank up, say, the kick and snare far beyond their normal level (relative to the rest of the mix) without busting your mixdown deck's headroom. Most models (both stereo and mono) can be linked in such a way that one unit acts as a master and the other a slave, maintaining a coherent stereo relationship.

If all of this has you feeling naked because you lack a compressor ("compressor envy," in Freudian terms), keep in mind that your gear inevitably does some compression in the course of its normal operation. Analog tape, in particular, is famous for its compression effect; experiment with recording at different levels, right on up to distortion, if you want to check it out. But if your home recordings are sounding jagged and unprofessional, a compressor might be just what you need to reach the next level of studio polish.

Fix It in the Mix

➤ What makes a good mix? As in most things musical, there's no one set of criteria. However, there are better mixes and worse mixes, and paying special attention to the mixdown stage of your productions can ensure that you end up with more of the former and fewer of the latter.

At the most basic level, the mixdown is to a recorded production what a conductor is to a live ensemble performance. In modern music, mixing is an extension of orchestration and arranging, and shares many of the same concerns. Let's examine some of the factors involved in creating an effective mix.

Keep in mind that these factors are not absolute values, but rather elements to be determined and manipulated for musical effect. For instance, maintaining sharp definition among various instruments, or constructing a convincing aural evocation of physical space, is only effective if it furthers the aesthetic aims of a given piece. The music may communicate more effectively with a muddled ensemble or an absence of spatial definition.

Definition. For most musicians, the bottom line is that every instrument be heard clearly (or, at least, that their own instrument be heard clearly). Mixes undertaken with this attitude tend to get the point across, but in a dull and insensitive fashion. Better to make sure that every *crucial* detail is clearly defined (the kick, snare, and vocal, say, in a rock song; the reverberant field in a new age piece), without losing sight of the other considerations discussed in this chapter. This is particularly true in a home studio, where, due to high noise floors and lack of proper tools, preserving subtle details can be difficult.

EQ can be used either to make room for an instrument by carving a place in the frequency spectrum out of the surrounding ensemble, or to enhance crucial overtones that will help it stand out. Compressing an instrument can allow you to place it up front while keeping its accents from popping out or overpowering the mix. Short reverberations ("room" programs) and very short delays can help bring an instrument closer to the front while keeping it from sounding as though it's simply laying over the top of the mix. Of course, too much reverb—a common problem—can make a mix so murky that nearly all definition is lost. Overly resonant or thick reverb can have the same result.

On the other hand, deliberately burying a sound in the mix can be quite effective. Just a little level, barely audible above a wash of reverb, can be enough to pique a listener's ear and evoke an entire world of sounds when only one is really there.

Proportion. A good mix usually achieves a balance of levels consistent with a sense of proportion among various instruments. A flute that's louder than the lead guitar doesn't sound natural, and isn't usually appropriate unless an unnatural sound is what you're after. In conventional rock practice, it's true, the snare drum is about the size of a

shopping mall while the vocalist stands about as tall as a high-rise apartment building, but listeners have become accustomed to hearing those particular exaggerations. Others just sound odd.

Try listening to various sonic elements in terms of how large they sound in relation to each other, and strive for a fairly realistic balance. With synthesized, heavily processed, or otherwise "unnatural" sounds, try to imagine their size in relation to the rest of the ensemble, and set their levels accordingly.

Dynamics. A song usually has obvious high and low points, in terms of overall level, which in most cases ought to be respected. For instance, the first verse probably shouldn't sound louder than the final chorus. Arrangements and orchestrations handle the bulk of dynamic variation in most music, but the mixing console can play a big role, too.

For instance, individual levels can come up during choruses and down during verses. EQ and effects can be switched in and out. A solo can begin softly and end blazing. Faders can be pushed slightly at the beginnings of phrases to call attention to instrumental entrances. Even if the song doesn't fade at the end, the master fader can be lowered gently to settle the mix into its final strains. This kind of dynamic motion imparts a breathing quality without which a mix can sound static and lifeless.

Naturally, faders can also be used to fix dynamics that weren't performed correctly. When an acoustic guitar's picking gets a little too exuberant during a quiet passage, pulling it down or rolling off some of the highs will bring it closer to its proper musical character.

Spatial Organization. Since contemporary music is usually recorded and often performed track by track, and eventually pumped out of a single pair of speakers, the sonic influence of the room in which the music was performed tends to be either confused or missing altogether. Reverbs, delays, and room microphones trained at the walls in order to pick up sonic reflections are used in conjunction with basic levels to reconstruct the lost impression of space. The space in which a piece of recorded music appears to take place can have a powerful musical effect.

Effect buses allow spatial simulations to be applied to any combination of instruments in a mix, making it possible to create an impression of several contrasting spaces at once. That is, the snare drum can reverberate as though it's in a concert hall (via a "hall" reverb program) while the vocalist appears to be contained in a small concrete chamber (quick delay with a little regeneration). An acoustic guitar can be strumming far off in the distance (very little dry signal, lots of wet signal) while the hi-hat seems to be only a few feet away (very little wet signal, lots of dry signal). Combinations are possible, as well. The vocalist in the concrete chamber can simultaneously be singing in the Grand Canyon (very long delay with regeneration sent to long reverb).

Reverb and delay can also be applied in such an exaggerated or mutated way that they lose their spatial implications, becoming sounds in and of themselves. Gated reverb is one example. Another is using a rather loud reverb return on one or two instruments to provide contrast in an otherwise dry mix.

Palette. This refers to the distribution of colors (*timbres*) in the mix, and naturally borders on arrangement and orchestration. From moment to moment, the colors should balance and/or complement each other, while over time the addition, subtraction, or modification of colors can add to the music's sense of drama or progression. EQ can bring each sound to its proper tint; other effects each lend their characteristic hue.

Feel. The difference between a mix that feels pretty good and one that feels perfect can be as tiny as a few half-dB level changes, a little bit of EQ, or a different reverb setting. Generally, every component sound should sit in the mix comfortably, so that it appears to be integrated with the ensemble. Sounds that seem to be apart from the ensemble can be massaged with level changes, EQ, reverb, delay, and other tricks of the trade until they blend well. Sometimes one sound simply won't mesh with the others, and the only thing to do is find another instrument, guitar tone, synthesizer patch, or whatever for the part and record it over again.

Magic. Even if you aren't quite ready to mix—some of the instruments or effects aren't set up yet, you don't have all of the fader/mute moves worked out, or whatever—the mix may feel outrageously good anyway. In this case, drop everything and get it on tape—it may never sound better. Then go back and finish for real. Respect magic when it shows its face in your studio.

Mixing By Numbers. Now that we've defined some of the qualities that make a good mix, it might be helpful to outline the process step-by-step. The following steps don't constitute an industry-approved method, but rather reflect my personal experience at the board. There's no right or wrong way to go about a mixdown. However, having a method is far preferable to simply throwing up the faders and trying to turn the resulting jumble of sounds into something coherent.

1. *Be prepared*. First things first. Place a strip of masking tape along the bottom of the console and label each fader with the name of its instrument. Likewise, label the effect sends, and any buses whose assignments you might have to think twice about. Set up basic effects in advance, and listen to make sure stereo effect returns are balanced on the right and left sides. Make sure your mixdown deck is receiving signals from the mixer's master outputs. Position your speakers so that they are evenly spaced and facing toward your ears. Clean all tape heads.

2. *Build a basic mix*. Isolate the essential elements that form the music's backbone. In a rock song, these are likely to be the kick, snare, and bass guitar, which usually pro-

vide a rhythmic and harmonic basis for every other instrument. If, perhaps due to lack of busing capabilities, you tend to route instruments directly through your reverb unit(s), make the relevant patches now and select a basic reverb setting. If your reverb is patched into an effects bus, add it after you've gotten a good basic blend.

Listen to each "backbone" instrument individually and apply EQ as necessary (or available). Then listen to them together, first panning them and then balancing their levels and fine-tuning the EQ until they blend nicely. Using a white grease pencil, mark the fader and pan settings so that you can get them back if you accidentally change them, or if you have to boost something temporarily.

Next, single out a few more elements that serve as direct support for the foundation. The rest of the drum kit fits into this category, as do the rhythm guitar and any rhythmic keyboard parts. Process these separately with EQ, flanging, and so forth. Then pan, balance, and re-EQ them in context with the basic parts, and add reverb and/or delay to taste. Now reassess all of the basic balances and tweak until the mix sounds unified. Mark (or re-mark) all pan locations and fader levels.

Pads and other lesser supporting parts, including hand percussion and counterlines, come next. Spiff up the mix by adding any interesting effects that come to mind, and be sure to mark all levels. Now it's time to add the lead instruments, establishing pan, EQ, fader, and effect settings.

Last, bring in the background vocals. Readjust settings as necessary.

3. *Listen.* By now everything should be sounding basically good. Before you go back for the fine points, listen to the entire song at high volume, and again at low volume. Find a comfortable compromise for the levels and reverb send amounts of any instruments that seem drastically different. Take a five-minute break and listen again, just to be sure.

4. *Choreograph the moves.* Having finalized the basic mix, determine and rehearse any "moves"—fader motions, EQ shifts, and so forth—that might be required. Note any fader levels that should change as the song plays, and practice moving them at the proper times and in the proper contours. Reverb sends may need to be attenuated for a solo; effects may need to be switched in and out. Mute or fade channels any time they're silent in order to lower the noise floor, bringing them back just before their instruments enter. An extra pair of hands—not to mention ears—can be invaluable at this stage, so invite a friend to help.

If the moves are particularly involved, you might do well to mix in sections and splice the pieces together (see the section on tape editing). This is possible only if you mix

to a reel-to-reel format, unless you're up for some gonzo cassette-to-cassette editing. Just mix until someone makes a mistake; stop the multi-track, rewind, and pick up where you left off. Save the cutting and pasting until you've gotten all of the way through, and don't, don't, don't unplug any patches, erase any markings, or move any EQ/effect settings until you've listened carefully to the spliced-together mix. Don't burn your bridges until you're sure you've crossed the river.

5. *Bounce carefully.* If you're using a 4- or 8-track tape deck, you can squeeze more instrumental parts onto the available tracks by filling up several tracks, mixing them to one (or two, for stereo), and then filling them up again with new parts. This is known as *bouncing.* (You might want to review the section on the subject, beginning on p. 92).

Bouncing is a sensible way around the limitations of the equipment, but it does limit your mixdown options. When you bounce tracks, you're forced to mix some musical elements before others have even been recorded. Experience and planning can minimize the guesswork involved, but you can't eliminate it altogether. Once the bounced tracks are mixed, they're set in stone.

The Ultimate Signal-Routing Solution: Designing and Building a Patch Bay

➤ The more devices you have in your studio, the harder it is to make efficient use of both your equipment and the time spent using it. It doesn't take a large number of signal processors, for instance, to tie up all of a mixer's busing capabilities. As you acquire processors in excess of this magic number, you spend more and more time crawling around behind your equipment racks plugging and unplugging cables.

It's possible to keep on top of this sort of situation, at least for a while, by working out a new routing scheme that accommodates your production methods. But eventually it becomes ridiculously impractical to keep everything wired up the same way all of the time.

The solution? A patch bay. That is, a simple panel of jacks, or *patch points*, each connected to an important input or output. Connections between jacks are made quickly and easily via short jumper cables called *patch cords* (see Fig. 4-14). A well-designed patch bay makes rearranging the distribution of any output to any input in your studio a fairly simple matter.

Building a bay that incorporates all of a relatively elaborate home studio's inputs and outputs can take a lot of

planning, time, money, soldering chops, and patience. However, creating a small one aimed at simplifying life in a small studio shouldn't take more than a few hours and a couple of hundred dollars.

Patch Bay Variables. Patch bays come in a variety of configurations. The variables are (1) how many jacks reside on each panel, (2) what kind of plugs the jacks accept, (3) whether the rear connections are made via plugs or solder connections, and (4) whether the jacks can be normalled (more on this later). The best arrangement for you depends on how extensive a bay you want and how much labor and money you're willing to put into it.

Generally speaking, the more jacks per panel, the better. (My *4-track* MIDI studio's patch bay consists of over 200 points—but I'm kind of a nut when it comes to this stuff.) Plug choices include mono 1/4" and RCA for unbalanced semi-pro studios, and bantam and full-sized ring-tip-sleeve for balanced, pro-level operations. Bantam is a good choice, since bantam plugs are small enough to allow around 100 jacks per single-rack-space panel. Unfortunately, they're expensive and can't be found at your local Radio Shack. In a semi-pro situation,

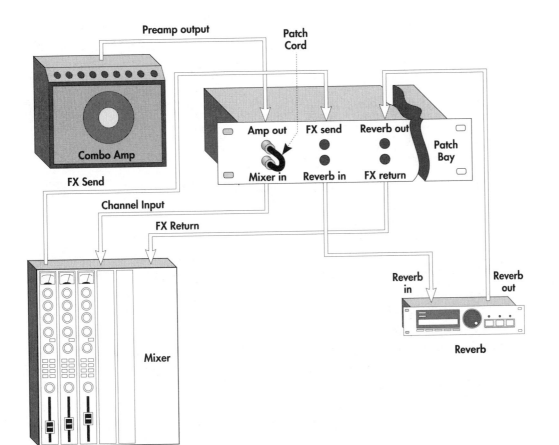

Preamp output

Patch Cord

Combo Amp

FX Send

Channel Input

FX Return

Amp out   FX send   Reverb out

Mixer in   Reverb in   FX return

Patch Bay

Mixer

Reverb in   Reverb out

Reverb

Fig. 4-14. A patch bay is simply a panel of jacks, or patch points, each connected to an important input or output. Connections between jacks are made via short jumper cables called patch cords. Outputs (usually the upper row of jacks) are best paired with related inputs (usually the lower row).

1/4" plugs are probably best because they're readily available, easy to solder (you'll probably need to make or repair patch cords from time to time), and relatively sturdy.

Plug-in rear connections tend to go along with semi-pro format jacks, while pro bays allow you to solder the jack-to-device connections. This makes sense, when you think about it: If you don't want to do any soldering, you can simply buy cables with the proper plugs long enough to reach from each input or output to the patch bay. This is fine for a small setup. With a larger, more complex rig, it becomes desirable to buy cable in bulk, cut the lengths to size, and solder the proper plug onto the

device end of each cable. Rather than solder a plug to the other end, it's only natural to attach it directly to the patch bay's rear.

Planning and Design. Planning is crucial if you want to end up with a patch bay that will make your studio as flexible as you need it to be. Start by making a list of all of the outputs in your studio: instruments, effects, mixers, tape decks, VCRs, turntables, radios, phone answering machines, and so forth. Then decide which you'd like to have access to at the patch bay—that is, which will need to be routed to more than one input in the course of production.

For instance, an equalizer's output may need to be routed to a multi-

Fig. 4-15. A normalled jack's internal switch is toggled whenever a plug is inserted.

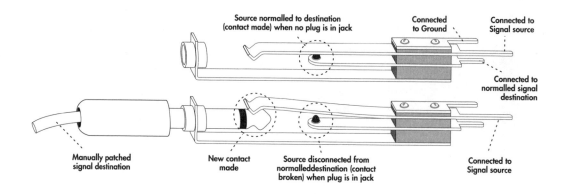

Source normalled to destination (contact made) when no plug is in jack

Connected to Ground

Connected to Signal source

Connected to normalled signal destination

Manually patched signal destination

New contact made

Source disconnected from normalleddestination (contact broken) when plug is in jack

Connected to Signal source

track input during the early stages of production, and to a mixer input during the mixdown phase. It would be more convenient to change the connections at the patch bay than to have to switch cables. On the other hand, if the only signals you'd ever route to your amp's auxiliary inputs are from the mixer's master outputs, then these connections might best be made with a pair of cables, bypassing the patch bay.

Repeat this process for all of your studio's inputs, including effects, amplifiers, mixers, tape decks, and so on. My tendency is to want to have *all* inputs and outputs available at the patch bay. Theoretically, this encourages novel applications and maximal use of each device. In many situations, however, this attitude is neither practical or cost-effective— cable, plugs, and soldering time add up.

Next, arrange the outputs and inputs to be included in the bay into useful pairs, with an output arranged above an input. You might want to think in terms of the most common connections (for instance, processor outputs above effect returns) or in

terms of simplicity (EQ outs above EQ ins). There is no standard way to arrange these pairs; it all depends on what you think will be most convenient.

Since patch bays are usually arranged as upper and lower rows of jacks, the layout you come up with, outputs above inputs, will be the template for your bay. Consistently placing outputs above inputs tends to keep the signal-flow apparent as the bay gets filled with patch cords.

Normalling. The next choice is which connections to *normal*. A normalled connection is one that doesn't need to be patched; the connection is made between two patch points internally, and is broken when a plug is inserted for an alternate routing (see Fig. 4-15). Normalled connections are useful because they (1) cut down on the time spent patching the same connections each time you work, (2) reduce clutter on the bay panel, and (3) conserve patch cords.

Normals can be a pain to wire up, but they're very handy. The ideal patch bay would be normalled into sort of a default configuration of the studio, making it possible to get a production underway with as few patches as possible. The next best thing is to normal those connections that are highly unlikely to change. This way, the inputs and outputs are available for rerouting, but most of the time you don't have to trouble yourself with them.

A Final Tip. If you do decide to install a patch bay in your studio, consider this tip: Build or buy a load of patch cords *first*. It's incredibly frustrating to get your wonderful new patch bay up and running, the ultimate solution to all of your signal-routing problems, only to find that you can't use the darn thing for want of a few bucks' worth of wire.

The Splice of Life: Tape-Editing Applications and Techniques

➤ As you probably know by now, analog tape is an endangered species. This is especially true in home studios. When it comes to multi-tracking, professional rooms concentrate on providing a large number of tracks, and although analog multi-track machines remain very expensive, they cost far less than their digital counterparts. At home, on the other hand, the tendency has been to eliminate conventional multi-track technology altogether by replacing it with virtual MIDI tracks and sampled sounds. And when it comes to mixdowns, there are a number of wonderful inexpensive non-analog alternatives. The days of analog, it seems, are numbered.

But when an old technology goes, many useful aspects of it go, too.

Sure, the new ways of doing things are smaller, cheaper, faster, more flexible, or all of the above. But they also make it hard to do things that were a snap in the old days. I'd like to spotlight a very important one: Tape editing.

One of the joys of analog tape is that you can rock it back and forth over the playback head until you hear the spot you're looking for, mark it with a grease pencil, lay it across a splicing block, cut it with a razor blade, and paste two loose ends together for a seamless, inaudible edit. You won't know just how useful this is until you've done it several times, but believe me, it comes in very handy. And in practical terms, you can't do it with anything but analog tape. The ability to do razor-

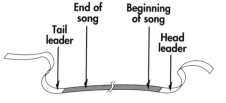

Fig. 4-16. Leadering the head and tail of each song on a reel eliminates extraneous sounds before and after the music, and makes it easy to locate individual songs.

blade edits is so useful that it makes sense to consider doing without digital and living with the higher noise floor, distortion, and inconvenience of analog.

Applications. The most mundane application of tape editing is tight-leadering each segment of music on a reel; that is, putting paper or plastic leader tape between each song (see Fig. 4-16). This way you can cut out unwanted sounds—tape hiss, count-offs, anticipatory noises—that precede the first note of music. Also, leader tape visually bands each piece of music, making it easy to find a particular song. Once the songs are leadered at head and tail, it's relatively easy to shuffle them into a master reel in the desired order and with the proper amount of silence (that is, leader tape) between each consecutive pair.

Editing becomes a creative tool when you consider using it to restructure a song. Perhaps it was a mistake to repeat that chorus at the end of your masterpiece; it's a snap to eliminate one repetition using a razor blade (see Fig. 4-17). On the other hand, you may regret that you didn't repeat the chorus once more; editing makes it easy to clone a chorus from elsewhere in the song and insert it. Similarly, you can chop out a mea-

sure, a few beats, even an electrical glitch (such as when your refrigerator turns on and wrecks the perfect mixdown).

Perhaps the most useful application of tape editing is as a sort of poor man's automation during a mixdown. If the mix has to go through radical changes, you can mix section by section, cutting the pieces together as you go. This requires some care if you want to achieve smooth transitions, since you have to make sure the ambient background of the music is more or less identical on either side of the splice, but it can save a lot of time.

And there are more creative possibilities: For instance, you can create dramatic disjunctures between one part of a song and the next. The ultimate realization of this approach is the "dance mix," which is often produced by mixing a song in a number of different ways and then intercutting the mixes for dramatic effect.

Technology. Editing tape is easiest if the equipment you're using is designed for it. Generally, the best tape format for editing a mixdown is half-track (two-channel) 1/4" running at 15 ips or faster. It's possible to edit wider formats and more tracks, even up to 2" 24-track, but it takes a bit more skill. Tape speed is important because at higher speeds the resolution is higher and the margin for error larger—that is, the sound is spread across a greater length of tape—but 7-1/2 ips will do in a pinch.

The tape deck itself should offer a few important features:

• The heads should be completely exposed, making it easy for you to reach the playback head with a grease pencil. (The hidden-head design is what makes cassettes virtually impossible to cut and paste with any accuracy.)

• A cue lever is crucial. This little item defeats the lifters that keep the tape out of contact with the heads when the machine isn't in record or play mode. When you're locating an edit point, the tape must be touching the playback head as you turn the reels by hand—otherwise, you won't be able to hear it.

• Some reel-to-reel decks provide a function called "edit mode." When it's engaged, the tape will play back even though it's not winding around the takeup reel—that is, when it's hanging loose on the right-hand side of the machine after having been cut. As it plays back in edit mode, the tape is dumped unceremoniously onto the floor, making it easy to play from the edit-out point to the edit-in point, cut the tape, join the two sides together, and discard the excess. If your machine lacks this function, you can achieve the same result by playing the tape while holding up the right-hand tension bar. (If you let go of the tension bar, the deck will stop.)

• Finally, a few incidental supplies are necessary. You'll need a box of old-fashioned single-edged razor blades, available at any hardware store. For marking the tape, a white grease pencil is best; you can get these from an art supply house. Finally, splicing tape or tabs and a

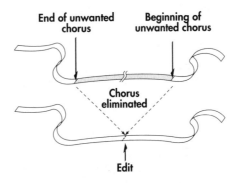

heavy-duty editing block, which you can find at a pro-audio store, are absolutely necessary.

Technique. We've taken a look at some of the reasons you might want to edit 2-track analog tape, the equipment required, and some of the features a good editing deck should have. But how do you do it? Assuming you have the necessary supplies and equipment in place, what follows is a step-by-step guide to tape editing.

You might want to practice on dubs of your favorite songs. Tight-leader a song. Remove a verse. Repeat a chorus. Create a stuttering cut-and-paste intro. Turn the tape backwards for a beat or two just before a dramatic transition. Once you get the hang of it, you'll find that mucking around with analog tape and razor blades is a lot of fun:

1. *Wash your hands.* Oil and dirt can accumulate on the tape as you handle it, causing high frequencies to drop out around the edit. If your hands are clean, you can handle the tape all you want. In fact, analog tape is remarkably hardy, and can take an amazing amount of abuse without any audible effect.

2. *Put the master reel on the tape*

Fig. 4-17. Tape editing opens up creative possibilities by making it possible to eliminate a segment of tape—for instance, an unwanted repetition of a chorus. Likewise, a chorus can be added, and unrelated segments of tape can be juxtaposed for interesting effects.

Fig. 4-18. Schematic representation of an edit in which the first of two verses is to be removed.

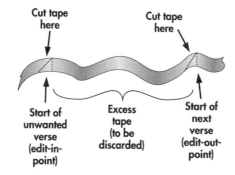

deck and assemble the relevant supplies:

• a white grease pencil for marking the edit points

• an unused single-edged razor blade for cutting the tape

• a roll of splicing tape for joining the loose ends

• leader tape for partitioning segments of tape

• a few spare empty reels for short-term storage of individual tape segments.

3. *Determine the edit-in and -out points,* the two places in the tape to be joined together (see Fig. 4-18). Choose carefully! Edit points should be easy to locate by ear and musically coherent, and they should create an appropriate-sounding transition (whether smooth or disjointed) when they're joined.

Prominent drum beats, such as kick and snare hits, often satisfy these criteria. They have an unambiguous sound that's easy to identify; they tend to occur in regular patterns, so it's usually not difficult to find edit-in and -out points that don't interrupt the musical flow; and the relative loudness of a drum's impact usually makes for a smooth transition. A kick drum at the beginning of the first and third verses,

immediately before the vocalist enters, for instance, would be a good choice. Vocal entrances, key changes, re-entrances after a pause, and other prominent textural shifts also tend to work.

4. *Locate the edit-in point on the tape and mark it.* This is where the most skill is involved. Different kinds of aural events sound different when you're rocking the tape back and forth over the playback head (as explained below). Recognizing them can take a bit of practice.

Start by playing the tape up to the edit-in point, stopping playback at the moment you hear it. Now, move the cue lever from its normal position to disengage the tape lifters. The tape should now be touching the playback head.

With one hand on each reel, pull the tape back and forth across the head and listen to the sounds recorded on it. When you pull the tape forward, you'll hear a short snippet of sound; when you pull it backward, you'll hear the same snippet in reverse. By rocking the tape back and forth, you should be able to zero in on the edit point.

Pull the tape past the spot at which you want to edit, and then back it up, taking care to back it up only to the very beginning and no farther. That's the essential technique: Pull the tape past the head until you hear what you're interested in, and back it up as far as necessary (see Fig. 4-19). If you've chosen an unambiguous musical feature, you should be able to locate its beginning with some accuracy. Try this a few

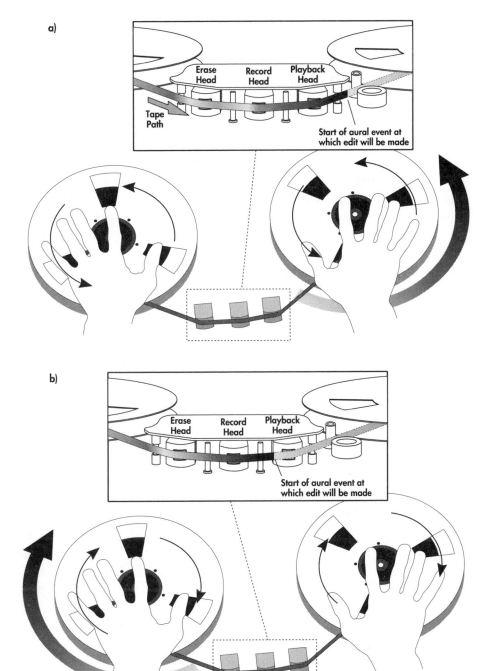

a)

b)

Fig. 4-19. The essential tape-editing technique: a) Holding one reel in each hand, twist the reels so that the tape moves forward past the playback head. b) When you hear the event at which you will edit, pull the tape backward so that the beginning of the event comes to rest slightly to the left of the playback head.

times; when you locate the edit point, play the tape to check your position. Do this until you develop some confidence.

When you think you've found the spot, mark the tape with a vertical line right down the middle of the playback head (see Fig. 4-20). Be sure not to mark the tape at the erase head or the record head! If you do,

Fig. 4-20. Mark the tape for editing with a vertical line right down the center of the playback head.

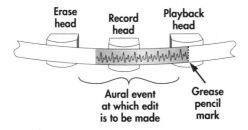

your edits will happen somewhere other than where you expect.

Once you've marked the tape, repeat the process to double-check yourself. This is worth doing, both in order to avoid making a mistake, and to develop consistency in the placement of your marks.

5. *Find the edit-out spot and mark it.* This is the same procedure you just performed with respect to the edit-in spot.

6. *Double-check both edit points for musical coherence.* Do this before you do any cutting. Listen not only for structural coherence—that is, that both edit points happen on, say, the third beat in a measure—but also for sonic coherence. The texture on either side of the edit should be consistent, and the reverberant field should be similar. Make sure you're not chopping off the reverb from a guitar solo just before the edit, or cutting into the reverb from the lead vocal in the verse that you've just excised.

7. *Rewind to the edit-in spot, place the tape in the splicing block, and cut it.* First, turn the takeup reel clockwise until the tape is loose enough to handle. Then, lay the tape flat in the splicing block with its backing (the side that doesn't touch the heads) up. Most blocks have two or three cut-

ting guides; use the one that describes a 45° angle.

Slide the tape in the block until the grease-pencil mark lies right below the upper edge of the cutting guide—you'll be cutting in front of the mark, not directly across it (see Fig. 4-21). Place one corner of your razor blade at the top of the guide, and pull it downward across the tape. Be careful to cut the tape in one motion so that the incision is straight, smooth, and tidy; it's difficult to work with a messy cut.

8. *Play through the excess tape.* To do this, it's necessary to take the left-hand side of the severed tape out of the splicing block. Pass it over the heads and between the capstan and pinch-roller.

If your machine has a switch labeled "edit" or "edit mode," press it now. This allows the tape to play back even though it's not winding around the takeup reel. If not, hold up the right-hand tension bar to achieve the same result.

Press play, and allow the excess tape between the edit points to pass across the deck and onto the floor to the right-hand side of the deck. When you hear (and/or see) the edit-out point pass, stop the tape.

9. *Place the tape in the splicing block at the edit-out point, and cut it.*

10. *Join the splice.* Pull the right-hand side of the newly severed tape out of the block. Don't let go of it yet, though; you'll need it if you've made a mistake and have to put the tape back together again. Using a piece of splicing tape, stick the loose end to the side of the tape deck so

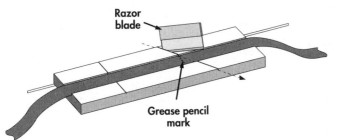

Razor
blade

Grease pencil
mark

Fig. 4-21. Place the tape in the splicing block with the grease-pencil mark positioned directly beneath the 45° cutting guide.

that it won't get lost.

At this point, the two ends of the edit should both be in the block. Butt the head and tail pieces together, and lay a small piece of splicing tape over the joint. (You can put the splicing tape on a corner of the razor blade, and use the blade as a handle to maneuver the splicing tape into position.) When the splicing tape is in place, smooth it with your finger.

11. *Play back your edit.* Make sure the edit button and the cue lever are back in their normal positions. Take the edited tape out of the splicing block and thread it over the heads and between the capstan and pinch-roller. Rewind a short distance, and take a listen.

12. *Enjoy.* If it sounds good, congratulations! You've made a successful tape edit.

If the edit sounds musically con-

tinuous but you hear a minor glitch, carefully remove the splicing tape, butt the ends together again, and reattach them. This often solves the problem.

If the edit sounds downright unmusical, you'll have to try again. Carefully remove the splicing tape. Find the loose end that you stuck to the deck and carefully reattach it to the left-hand side of the unfortunate edit. By hand, rewind the excess tape that piled up on the floor. Reattach the remaining loose ends, and return to Square One. The tape shouldn't sound any worse for wear.

Making good edits requires a reasonable amount of experience, practice, and care, but once you're comfortable with it, it's really quite easy. And you're sure to find the creative and practical benefits well worth the effort that it takes to learn.

Gain-Staging Your Studio

➤ Whenever a signal in your studio is amplified, it passes through circuitry called a *gain stage*. The amplifier that boosts your mixer's master outputs to a level that your speakers can work with is only the most obvious one. Preamplifiers—basically amplifiers with less muscle—are gain stages, too.

Most likely, there's an input preamp at the head of every input channel of your mixer. Most signal-processing devices feature an input-level control, which is also a preamp. Synthesizers and samplers usually have preamps at their outputs in the form of a master volume control. A tape deck's level controls count, too.

Why so many gain stages? Because every device that accepts an input has an optimal input level at which it performs at highest fidelity and best signal-to-noise ratio. Weak signals must be cranked up, and strong signals have to be attenuated. Building a gain stage into a device's input and/or output circuitry allows this to be done cleanly and conveniently.

But there's a cost to the control that gain stages provide. A signal is degraded slightly with each one it passes through. A little noise creeps in, and possibly some harmonic and inharmonic distortion—but presumably much less than if the gain could

only be boosted or cut at the end of the signal chain. The recording engineer's job is to adjust all of the various gain stages so that noise and distortion are kept to a minimum.

Naturally, this is easier said than done. Aside from the complexity of managing all of the signals flying around a large recording system, signal levels are in constant fluctuation. An acoustic guitar may be quiet one moment and very loud the next. How do you keep signals at the right levels when they're changing all the time?

Max Headroom. Compression is one answer, but a more general one is *headroom*. Having decided upon a nominal operating level for a piece of gear (0dB), manufacturers build in a few dB of tolerance, or headroom, above this level before clipping sets in. Signals that stay within this range are likely to escape distortion-free. Building in headroom doesn't keep signals at their best levels, but it ensures that they operate in the range that provides the best signal-to-noise ratio without becoming too hot to handle.

Headroom is a critical issue during a mixdown, when signals pass through several gain stages in a row. Typically, a signal entering a mixer passes through at least three of them:

an input preamp, a channel fader, and the fader(s) for the stereo master-output bus. Here's how you can set them up to allow approximately 10dB of headroom, regardless of how much the manufacturer has built in.

Calibrating A Mixer. All it takes is a sine wave generator that produces a 1kHz tone at -10dB (if you work with semi-pro equipment) or +4dB (for pro gear) and a VU meter, preferably a free-standing one. If you're not sure about the nominal operating level of your equipment, check the manual's specification page. If you don't have access to a free-standing meter, route the tone to a tape deck and adjust its input level control so that the meter reads 0dB—that is, so that -10dB (with semi-pro gear) or +4dB (with pro gear) coming from the tone generator equals 0dB on the meter.

1. Set the tone generator to the proper level for your equipment. Route the 1kHz tone to the VU meter, just to make sure it's reading close to 0dB. Don't worry too much if it's not exactly 0dB. That simply means that the tone generator is inaccurate or the meter is out of calibration—probably the latter. Because levels are in constant flux, under real-world conditions your gain staging will never be exact anyway.

2. Route the tone to the mixer's first input channel. Bring up the channel's fader, the master faders, and the monitor level so that you can hear the tone clearly. The exact fader positions aren't important at this point.

3. Turn the input preamp fully down, and begin to turn it slowly clockwise. When it's somewhere beyond halfway up, you should hear the tone distort; the pure sine wave will suddenly become edgy and begin to sound like a square wave. At this point, you've exceeded the headroom of the input preamp. Back it up to the point just before distortion sets in.

4. Route the channel's *direct output* to the meter and note the level. Back off the preamp (not the fader) until the meter reads exactly 10dB less. The input preamp is now calibrated to provide 10dB of headroom.

5. Now, place the fader at the 0dB mark (which represents 0 boost or cut at the fader), or at the top of the shaded range. Make sure the channel is panned center. Note the level displayed by the channel's own meter. (It should be between -10dB and 0dB.) Pick the nearest dB increment, and, using the preamp pot, adjust the level until the meter reads that value exactly.

6. Repeat the procedure for each channel, adjusting each to the dB value you selected in step 5.

7. After calibrating the last channel, leave its fader up, make sure it's panned center, and raise the master faders until the master bus meters read the same level as the individual channel's meter. Mark this position, and consider it the best location for the master faders during a mixdown.

When a session requires the use of several mixer channels at once, consider the *lower* end of the each fader's shaded range to be the 0dB mark. At the upper end of the shaded range, *a single fader* sends signal to the master bus with 0dB of gain. The lower end of the shaded range represents the level at which *the sum of all faders* produces 0dB of gain at the master bus.

It's not a bad idea to kick off your most serious production sessions by "zeroing" the console in this manner. In the real world, some of the signals you route to your mixer's input channels will be too low and others will be too high. If you find that you need more level than a channel's fader provides—that is, the input signal is too low—get it by boosting the preamp a bit. You can consider an input signal too hot if you hear the channel breaking up. Otherwise, you can run your session secure in the knowledge that you're getting the best practical signal-to-noise ratio and lowest distortion your mixer is capable of.

Expanding Your Studio With MIDI, Computers, and Virtual Tracks

➤ If you use drum machines, synthesizers, or samplers—that is, MIDI instruments—one of the most powerful ways to upgrade your studio is to employ *virtual tracks*. "Virtual" is computerese for "not existing in fact, but existing in function, thanks to a computer." In other words, virtual tracks reside not on tape, but in a computer running a software application commonly known as a MIDI sequencer.

Practically speaking, you lose one track of tape to a synchronization signal, and gain as many tracks as you have MIDI instruments. A 4-track setup can be converted very handily into 19 or more, although the additional tracks are necessarily dedicated to electronic sounds. The signal routing involved is illustrated in Fig. 4-22.

Assembling such a system from scratch involves relatively large-scale finances and a working knowledge of MIDI, but if you already have some MIDI gear and a computer, you're halfway there. (If not, you may have just discovered where all of your free time and money will go well into the next decade.) Basically, the necessary components are a sequencer, some sort of synchronizer, a MIDI controller, MIDI-controlled sound gener-

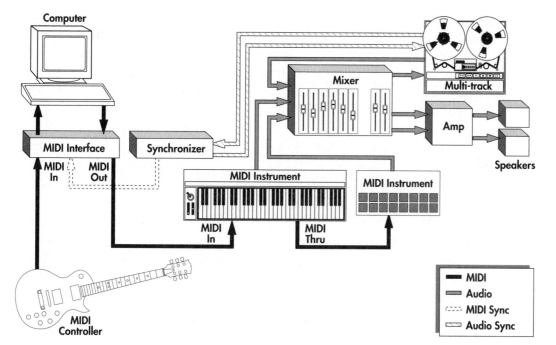

Fig. 4-22. Signal routing for a system employing virtual tracks: Audio signals are represented by light lines, MIDI signals by dark lines, and sync signals by dotted lines.

ators, and enough mixer input channels to accommodate the additional "tracks."

• *Sequencer.* MIDI sequencers come in dozens of shades, but the three basic categories are software, dedicated hardware, and integrated. Software, of course, runs on a personal computer. Good sequencers exist for IBM, Apple, Atari, and Commodore models. If you're new to MIDI sequencing, you might want to start with a program designed for beginners. If you have anything but an Atari, you'll also have to buy a MIDI interface, which converts the MIDI data into a format the computer can deal with.

Dedicated-hardware sequencers integrate the computer, the interface, and the software into a single, compact box. In many cases, this is the simplest, most economical way to go; it's certainly the best choice for

sequencer-based live performance. Hardware sequencers, however, lack the large-screen display that computer users take for granted, and are less readily updated with new features.

Integrated sequencers are built into the "workstation" variety of MIDI instrument. Machines such as the Korg M-1 incorporate a sequencer, samples, synthesis, effects, rudimentary mixing, and a MIDI keyboard controller in one unit at a very reasonable price. Integrated sequencers may not have the ability to lock up to an external sync tone—essential for virtual tracking— so make sure this function is available before you sink your savings into one of these babies.

• *Synchronizer.* Synchronization keeps the sequencer informed about the current position of the multi-track tape, so that the two can record and play back together. The sync functions we're talking about here—sync tone generation and conversion of the tone into MIDI timing information—come either in a stand-alone box or built into a MIDI interface.

Different sequencers may require different kinds of sync signals, but today the de facto standard is SMPTE. The basic procedure is to record SMPTE (an audio sync tone generated by the sync box) onto one track of the multi-track before you begin making music. When the sync tone is played back into the synchronizer, it generates a MIDI timing signal based on the current SMPTE time. (At least one tape deck on the market synchronizes its motor directly to an input SMPTE signal, saving the track otherwise dedicated to sync. However, it also changes the nature of the system I'm describing.) There are two MIDI timing formats, MIDI time code (MTC) and song position pointers (SPP). Before you buy, make sure the synchronizer generates the format that your sequencer reads. If you have a choice, MTC is the better way to go.

• *MIDI controller*. This generates the MIDI control information that the sequencer memorizes, and that drives drum machines, synthesizers, and samplers, just like a guitar generates the sound your tape deck records. For the most part, MIDI controllers mimic traditional instruments: keyboards, guitars, drums, clarinets, and violins.

The state of the technology in guitar controllers still dictates that you adapt your playing technique a bit, but so does the difference between acoustic and electric guitars, so it shouldn't be such an alarming prospect. Nonetheless, many guitarists find it simpler to use keyboard- and drum-style controllers.

• *MIDI-controlled sound generators*. These include drum machines, synths, and samplers—the more, the merrier. The number of effective virtual tracks available depends not on the number of tracks offered by the sequencer (often dazzlingly high), but on the number of MIDI channels—usually 16, but often 32, and conceivably more—and the number of different sounds, also called *patches* and in this context *timbres*, your stable of instruments can produce at one time.

Drum machines are necessarily *multi-timbral* (that is, able to produce several sounds at once), since they have to produce snare, kick, cymbal, and percussion sounds at once to simulate a live drummer and additional percussionists. Although many new synths and samplers are still mono-timbral, multi-timbral units are becoming standard fare. Generally, the more independent, simultaneous timbres an instrument provides, the more flexibility and bang for the buck it offers. The downside is increased complexity of operation, and of the system itself, as various sounds must be allocated to instrument voices and routed from individual instrument outputs to mixer inputs.

• *Mixer input channels*. In a 4-track system, five or six mixer channels

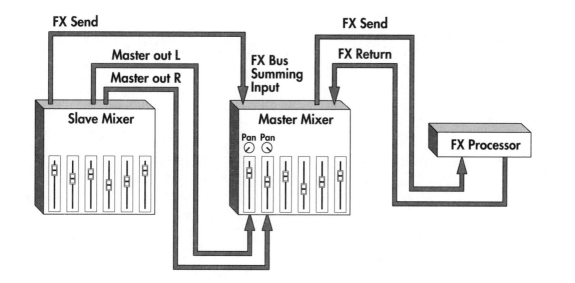

Fig. 4-23. Connecting two mixers to share outboard effects: The stereo output of the slave mixer is routed to two channels of the master mixer. The slave's effect sends are summed with those of the master, while the effects are returned via the master's returns or input channels.

(not counting effect returns) will suffice: one for each tape track, one for adding an instrument during mixdown, and one for good measure. In a medium-sized MIDI system, the number of necessary channels can be kept down to, say, 12 or 16 by using each multi-timbral instrument's mix output. On the other hand, if you want individual control over each sound, you're going to need a mixer channel for each. Taking this approach, it's not difficult to fill 24

channels or more in even a small, but timbre-intensive, system.

Fortunately, inexpensive line-level mixers sporting large numbers of input channels are available for just such applications. If you don't want to trash your current mixer, look for a board that can be strapped onto the system. This generally requires *summing inputs* for the effect buses, so that the old and new mixers run in tandem, sharing the same effect units (see Fig. 4-23).

Peak Performance: An Engineer/Producer's Guide

➤ It takes more than expertise and a pile of high-tech gear to make a great recording. Another essential ingredient is a great performance. Although that part of the job is in the hands of each musician—who, in a home studio, is likely to be the engineer wearing a few different hats—there are a number of things a recording engineer/producer can do to help the players on his or her recording deliver a peak performance.

Metronomes. The simplest performance aid is a click track—simply a metronome that keeps everybody together, or keeps the one-man band in time with himself as he records successive overdubs (see Fig. 4-24). Before you begin recording, determine the ideal tempo for the song and stripe one track of tape with a metronome at that tempo—and don't forget to play it back in "sync" mode as you record new tracks! If you're using tape sync and MIDI instruments, synthesize the metronome's sound and save a precious track of tape. If you have a drum machine, the players might prefer a rudimentary drum part to a lifeless click.

If the song has an intro that's played freely, keep the metronome silent until two beats before the moment strict time sets in. This gives the players a proper cue. Likewise with endings; be sure to pull the metronome out at the right moment. Also, it can be very annoying to hear a click when it isn't necessary, particularly during playback of a completed take. Be aware of the metronome's level at all times, and pull it out when it isn't necessary.

A final caveat: While attempting to keep the band sounding tight, it's easy to forget that from a musical point of view, a metronome isn't always appropriate. Although most popular music maintains a steady tempo, metronomic time can be so rigid that the music doesn't seem to breathe and flow. Also, musicians can be distracted in their efforts to follow the metronome and fail to get locked into the groove. Moreover, many kinds of music don't keep a steady tempo. These either require a special *rubato* click track, or must be performed without one.

Guide Tracks. A variation on the metronome is the guide track. In a live band situation, each player sees and hears the others; the musicians can respond to each other as they play. In a multi-track recording, on the other hand, the musicians play along with pre-recorded tracks. They can't interact with each other, often making the performance flat and life-

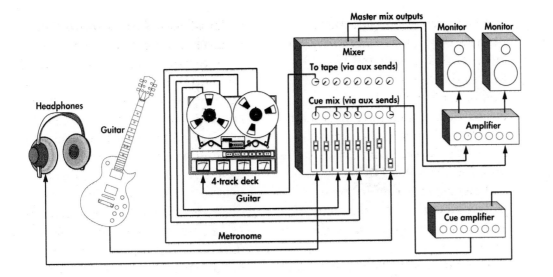

Master mix outputs

Mixer

To tape (via aux sends)

Cue mix (via aux sends)

Monitor   Monitor

Amplifier

Headphones

Guitar

4-track deck

Guitar

Metronome

Cue amplifier

Fig. 4-24. Using a metronome for improved performances: A click track, generated by a metronome or drum machine, is recorded on one track of tape. Its signal is added to the cue mix and sent to the musicians' headphones. The metronome is kept out of the mixer's master outputs (note fader levels).

less. The solution is to start with a track that isn't intended to be part of the final product, but lets everybody know where they are in the song, or what they should be doing: a big tom-tom fill leading into the chorus, say, or a simple chordal part that articulates every quarter-note.

Background vocals can benefit a lot from this technique. Sometimes vocalists singing in harmony have trouble keeping their first note in mind; if they hear it just before their entrance, they'll hit it every time. An arpeggiated chord, making each individual note obvious, works like a charm. Likewise, recording an *a cappella* vocal passage can be much easier if the singers are listening to the chords on a separate track. (Of course, the guide need not be recorded; it can be played in real time during each take if you need to save a track.)

A spoken guide track can also be useful. For example, if you plan to overdub a guitar solo that's intended to build to a climax over a long

period of time, record a count of each bar as it passes. Even though they aren't playing along with your solo, the musicians will know to cool out until bar 46, and that by the time they get to bar 78 they should be having a full-bore rave-up. If the song's dynamics are particularly involved, you can record a track in which you explain—succinctly, of course—that it should get a little louder, still louder, even louder, crash—or whatever else is appropriate.

The Cue Mix. In many recording situations, the players hear each other only through headphones. Thus, the mix sent to their cans—called the *cue mix*, or the *monitor mix*—is critical. First and foremost, each player needs to be able to hear him- or herself. The degree is a matter of personal preference; some musicians want their own sound to dominate, while others want to concentrate on the other instruments.

Players also need to hear instruments related to the part they're playing. Rhythm guitarists may need an extra dose of kick and snare to lock into the groove. Singers often sing better if they're hearing an unmistakable pitch reference, such as a combination of bass and a keyboard pad. Interlocking rhythmic figures, such as funky keyboard, guitar, and percussion parts, are easier to perform if their levels are balanced and the sounds are spread across the stereo field.

Beyond these considerations, the monitor mix ought to sound *good*. It should be inspiring. It doesn't need to be as finely honed as a final mix, but it should be far enough along that it has a life of its own. Don't spare the reverb, delay, and other effects—they can really help a performer get into the music.

Emotional Atmosphere. The studio is a tinderbox of both creativity and egomania. The perceived talent, and thus self-worth, of everyone involved is on the line at one time or another. Tensions can rise and fall with alarming speed and frequency. Depending on the personalities of those involved, some tensions are helpful, others destructive.

Be aware that the emotional atmosphere can be a determining factor in the effectiveness of every musician's performance. Be liberal with your enthusiasm. Maintain an attitude of cooperation and supportiveness. Make everyone feel that their efforts are valuable, and let them know when they hit the nail on the head. Once the momentum develops, keep it going. Everyone in the studio will notice the difference.

Recording Great Guitar Sounds

➤ Electronic instruments such as synthesizers, samplers, and drum machines are fairly easy to record. Guitars, however, present special problems. Acoustic guitars exhibit subtleties that are easily missed by a microphone and tape deck. They aren't as "present," and are easily overpowered in a mix with electric instruments. Electric guitars are usually less subtle, but they're expected to hold their own against such powerful contenders as bass and drums, and are often required to fill up most of the space in a recording with buzzing, jangling, glittering excitement. Pretty tall orders.

By now, we've covered just about all of the basic concepts and techniques involved in recording great guitar sounds, so let's round them up and examine them in light of this specific application. Below, I've tried to identify a number of factors that can make or break recorded guitar sounds. Most of them apply equally to recording any acoustic instrument, or any instrument that depends on vibrating air for its sound. By considering each one in turn as you work, you should be able to upgrade the quality of your productions. The best part is, your guitars will sound magnificent.

As always, success in this endeavor depends a great deal on your ears. They provide you with the sense of discrimination to know when the sound is perfect and when it needs more work—and in that case, what it will take to make it perfect. If things aren't great and don't seem to be improving, don't be afraid to pull out all of the patch cords, take a break, and start again from scratch—sometimes that can make all the difference, and it rarely makes things worse. Always keep your ears open for an opportunity to improve the sound, and respect the opinions of others who may hear more clearly than you.

1. *The source.* Sound, transduced into electrical energy, follows a signal path that leads from its source, the guitar, through various routing and processing devices—patch bays, equalizers, etc.—to its ultimate destination, the recording medium (i.e., tape). Each link in the chain between source and tape is a potential cause of distortion, but in absolute terms the chain itself can only be as good as the source.

Translated into plain English, the message is: Make sure the guitar itself sounds good—an acoustic guitar's tone in the air, an electric guitar's from its amplifier. If the instrument and the player are both happening, then your job is simply to capture the beauty. If the guitar stinks, it's up to you to de-emphasize offensive portions of the audio spectrum and emphasize those that sound right (or, if things are bad enough, to blur the sonic image to the degree that the defects aren't really noticeable).

2. *Miked or direct?* With electric guitars, you have the option of recording via a microphone trained on the amp, or processing the guitar's signal through any number of electronic effects and routing the final output directly to the tape deck. The latter choice, going direct, simplifies recording a great deal. Unfortunately, it also eliminates the sonic complexities otherwise added by the vibrating speaker, the room, and the microphone. These often contribute such intangible elements as presence, guts, and punch which you may not want to do without. If they're missing from the direct feed, you'll have to create them using such effects as delay and overdrive distortion. There's no clear-cut way to decide; it depends on your equipment, ears, and abilities.

3. *The room.* The room comes into play any time you're using a microphone rather than going direct. Sound bouncing off the walls is picked up by the mike along with sound coming directly from the instrument or amp, making the sound wetter (more diffuse) or drier (more focused). Generally, hard surfaces such as concrete, glass, and

wood reflect a lot of sound, while softer surfaces, especially curtains and rugs, absorb sound.

If you're in a room that's too reverberant, particularly if it has a pronounced resonance—it's easy to check by clapping your hands and listening for the pitch of the echo—put some blankets over the floor, walls, and windows. If the room is too dry, pull up the rug and empty the room of furniture.

The less reflected sound your mike picks up, the more carefully you can tailor the reverberant environment artificially by mixing in reverb, delays, and so forth. On the other hand, naturally reflected sound can have a nice lively quality. It may be part of the quality you want to capture—somewhat more difficult to do, by the way.

If the room's own sound isn't just right as it's picked up by the mike, you'll have to find a way to isolate it. Train a mike on the walls or corners to pick up predominantly reflected sound. This allows you to control how much of it gets into the mix.

Another variable has a lot of influence over how much "room sound" gets into your recordings, namely:

4. *Microphone position.* The basic rule of mike placement is: Use your ear. Treat your ear as though it's a mike. Move it around the room and see what it picks up. As you might expect, the best place for a microphone is usually more or less directly in front of the soundhole—but you never know until you experiment with other positions.

Sometimes the best way to get rid of boominess or dullness (two very common problems) is to move the microphone a few inches to the left or right, or forward or backward, or up or down. It can take some time and a lot of listening to find the best spot. If you've exhausted your patience with the mike, don't despair; there's always EQ (see below).

Generally, close placement gives you a drier sound; distant miking gives you a wetter, more ambient sound. Stereo miking techniques are great for recording solo guitar, since they maintain some semblance of the actual ambience of the room during the performance. For rock and roll, you're probably better off adding artificial stereo ambience to a close-miked sound.

5. *Microphone choice.* Most home studios don't offer much choice in this department. It's tempting to use the same Shure SM-57 you use to mike your Marshall stack onstage, but a more sensitive mike—one that couldn't stand that kind of abuse—can make a big difference. Condenser mikes, which tend to be more sensitive to high-frequency transients than dynamic mikes, are ideal for acoustic guitars, but they're also more fragile and expensive, and they require phantom power. At home, a mid-to-high-quality dynamic, such as a Beyer M88, will usually suffice.

Acoustic guitarists often resort to a contact mike, a pickup that attaches directly to the face of the instrument, in order to avoid having to stand in one place. A contact mike can be very useful in recording, as well. It can be used as the sole source of a guitar's recorded sound, or mixed with the signal from a regular microphone. For an interesting variation, try contact-miking your acoustic, amplifying it with a tube amp such as a Fender Twin, and miking the amp. This can add a lot of interesting coloration.

My final suggestion is a little odd, but I've heard it produce great results for acoustic guitarists: Put the mike *inside* the instrument. How the heck do you get a microphone inside a guitar? Well, if the mike is small enough—a *lavalier*, or lapel, mike of the kind used by broadcasters—you can pass it behind the strings and let it dangle just inside of the sound-hole, taping the wire to the instrument if necessary. Radio Shack sells cheap lavaliers, so it's not expensive to experiment with this technique.

6. *Signal processing.* This is *tres* important. Once you've captured the sound to the best of your own, and your equipment's, abilities, it's time to shape it into the sound you're looking for. The basic bag of tricks: distortion, compression, equalization, brightening (from an exciter or similar device), and delay. In a home studio, you'll probably want to use this stuff before the signal gets to tape, rather than in the mix. Remember that slight changes in equalization, delay time, and the like can make a lot of difference in the studio.

• A compressor keeps the guitar's level within a range that's acceptable to your tape machine, as well as appropriate to the musical context in which it will be heard. A solo classical guitar may require very little compression. Add a lead vocal, though, and the guitar (as well as the voice) often needs to be reined in so that it can be placed up front in the mix without overpowering the vocalist with every vigorous stroke.

In a rock and roll context, you might want to bear down on acoustic guitars so that you can keep them back without losing the quieter strokes. Electric guitars are nearly always squashed; clean sounds less so, distorted sounds more so.

• EQ is the right tool for eliminating any oddball bumps or dips in the frequency spectrum—boominess, dullness, harshness, and so on.

• A little extra brightness can bring out a guitar's ringing quality and add definition. Exciters and enhancers are usually better for this than EQ because they can do the job without adding much high-frequency noise.

• A short delay, in the chorusing range but without any LFO modulation, can add fullness, particularly when the processed and unprocessed versions of the signal are panned in stereo. Careful with this one on acoustic guitar, though—it's easy to lose the natural, non-electric quality. A tiny bit goes a long way.

• A medium delay, somewhat on the order of a perceptible slap-back, brings out the chunkiness of grooving rhythm parts.

• A long delay in the duration of a quarter-note or more can add elegance and fullness to lead lines. Regeneration adds a ponderous quality. Experiment with delays that are in and out of time with the music.

7. *Arrangement.* In a live setting, multiple guitars—acoustic or electric—aren't particularly impressive. But in a multi-track recording, where you can tweak each one especially for its musical role with EQ, delays, reverb, and so forth, the results can be heavenly. Arrange the guitars for a strumming part, a picking part, a high part, a single-note low part, etc., and then mix them so they each have a distinctive identity. In the realm of recorded sounds, this one is hard to beat.

8. *Mixdown.* This is where it all comes together, and it can have a big influence on how your sounds appear to the listener. The mix is a time for putting the guitar in perspective; making it the "size" you think it ought to be, making it sound natural or processed, giving it a context within the ensemble's right-to-left and front-to-back positioning. If the guitar is supposed to be the center of attention, mix it so that it *demands* that attention. If it's supposed to hang in the background and provide atmosphere, mix it to do that job.

Don't worry if the mixdown requires more time than it took to record the tracks. It's common enough, and sometimes appropriate, for a mix to take more than one day. *Always* keep a reel of tape in the machine to capture that magic moment when all of the faders, effects sends, and other settings suddenly fall into perfect harmony of their own accord (it happens from time to time).

On the other hand, don't hesitate to tear the mix apart and start from scratch if it's not happening. Be patient. Give yourself plenty of room to stretch out, listen, experiment, and realize your ideal mix.

Index

Also available from Miller Freeman

Acoustic Guitars and Other Fretted Instruments: A Photographic History
George Gruhn and Walter Carter
A lavishly illustrated book telling the story of American fretted instruments from the 1830s to the present. The evolution and sibling rivalry is traced, Features hundreds of unique color photographs of acoustic guitars, mandolins, and banjos.
ISBN 0-87930-240-2 $39.95

All Music Guide: The Best CDs, Albums & Tapes
Edited by Michael Erlewine and Scott Bultman
Reviews the best recordings in twenty-six musical categories including classical, rock, gospel, country, rap, and jazz and a total of 23,000 listings. This is the guide for everyone who's walked into a music store and felt overwhelmed by "what to choose?"
ISBN 0-87930-264-X $19.95

The Musician's Guide to Reading & Writing Music
Dave Stewart
For the brand new rocker, the seasoned player, and the pro who could use new problem-solving methods, a clear and practical guide to learning written music notation.
ISBN 0-87930-273-9 $7.95

Bass Heroes:
Styles, Stories & Secrets of 30 Great Bass Players
Edited by Tom Mulhern
Thirty of the world's greatest bass players in rock, jazz, studio/pop, and blues & funk share their musical influences, playing techniques, and opinions. Includes Monk Montgomery, Jack Bruce, James Jamerson, Stanley Clarke, Paul McCartney, and many more. From the pages of *Guitar Player* magazine.
ISBN 0-87930-274-7 $17.95

Vintage Synthesizers:
Groundbreaking Instruments and Pioneering Designers of Electronic Music Synthesizers
Mark Vail
Focuses on the modern history (1962-1992) of the electronic synthesizer, including in-depth interviews with pioneering synth designers and users, performance techniques, buying tips, and production and pricing information.
ISBN 0-87930-275-5 $17.95

Secrets from the Masters: 40 Great Guitar Players
Edited by Don Menn
Featuring the most influential guitarists of the past 25 years: Chuck Berry, Joe Satriani, Eddie Van Halen, John Scofield, Pete Townshend and many more. Combines personal biography, career history, and playing techniques. From the pages of *Guitar Player* magazine.
ISBN 0-87930-260-7 $19.95

The Fender Book:
A Complete History of Fender Electric Guitars
Tony Bacon and Paul Day
Tells the complete story of these hugely popular, versatile, and fascinating guitars, from the classic 1950s Telecaster and Stratocaster to current models. Illustrated with unique color photographs of outstanding and unusual Fender models.
ISBN 0-87930-259-3   **$19.95**

Gruhn's Guide to Vintage Guitars: An Identification Guide for American Fretted Instruments
George Gruhn and Walter Carter
This portable reference for identifying American guitars, mandolins, and basses contains comprehensive dating information and model specifications for nearly 2,000 instruments by all major U.S. manufacturers.
ISBN 0-87930-195-3 $22.95

Guitar Player Repair Guide: How to Set Up, Maintain, and Repair Electrics and Acoustics
Dan Erlewine
Whether you're a player, collector, or repairperson, this hands-on guide provides all the essential information on caring for guitars and electric basses. Includes 264 photos and drawings.
ISBN 0-87930-188-0 $19.95

The Gibson Super 400: Art of the Fine Guitar
Thomas A. Van Hoose
This book traces the evolution of the Gibson 400 including production details and tables, historical anecdotes, step-by-step restoration techniques, and pricing information. Numerous color and black and white photographs make this volume complete.
ISBN 0-87930-230-5 $49.95

The Musician's Home Recording Handbook: Practical Techniques for Recording Great Music at Home
Ted Greenwald
An easy-to-follow, practical guide to setting up a home recording studio for all musicians who want to get the best results from the equipment at hand.
ISBN 0-87930-237-2 $19.95

Blues Guitar: The Men Who Made the Music
Edited by Jas Obrecht
"These pieces get straight to the blues through the eyes of the men who lived it."—*Los Angeles Times*. Interviews, articles, discographies, and rare photographs of 25 of history's greatest bluesmen, including Robert Johnson, John Lee Hooker, Albert King, B.B. King, Buddy Guy, Muddy Waters and many more.
ISBN 0-87930-187-2 $19.95

CyberArts: Exploring Art & Technology
Edited by Linda Jacobson
A rich anthology of essays and commentaries from over 50 leading multimedia visionaries on the topics of music, graphics, animation, 3D sound, virtual reality, video and film, toys, and games.
ISBN 0-87930-253-4 $22.95

TO ORDER, or for more information, contact:
Miller Freeman Books, 600 Harrison St., San Francisco, CA 94107
Phone 415 905-2200 • Fax 415 905-2239.